KILL RO

Operation *Flipper* 1941

GAVIN MORTIMER

First published in Great Britain in 2014 by Osprey Publishing,
PO Box 883, Oxford, OX1 9PL, UK
PO Box 3985, New York, NY 10185-3985, USA
E-mail: info@ospreypublishing.com

Osprey Publishing is part of the Osprey Group

A CIP catalogue record for this book is available from the British Library

Print ISBN: 978 1 4728 0109 8
PDF ebook ISBN: 978 1 4728 0110 4
ePub ebook ISBN: 978 1 4728 0111 1

Index by Fionbar Lyons
Typeset in Sabon
Maps by bounford.com
3D BEV by Alan Gilliland
Originated by PDQ Media, Bungay, UK
Printed in China through Worldprint Ltd

14 15 16 17 18 10 9 8 7 6 5 4 3 2 1

Osprey Publishing is supporting the Woodland Trust, the UK's leading
woodland conservation charity, by funding the dedication of trees.

www.ospreypublishing.com

IMPERIAL WAR MUSEUM COLLECTIONS

Many of the photos in this book come from the Imperial War Museum's
huge collections which cover all aspects of conflict involving Britain
and the Commonwealth since the start of the twentieth century. These
rich resources are available online to search, browse and buy at
www.iwmcollections.org.uk . In addition to Collections Online, you can visit
the Visitor Rooms where you can explore over 8 million photographs,
thousands of hours of moving images, the largest sound archive of its kind
in the world, thousands of diaries and letters written by people in wartime,
and a huge reference library. To make an appointment, call (020) 7416
5320, or e-mail mail@iwm.org.uk .

Imperial War Museum www.iwm.org.uk

ARTIST'S NOTE

Readers may care to note that the original paintings from which the
battlescenes of this book were prepared are available for private sale.
All reproduction copyright whatsoever is retained by the Publishers. All
enquiries should be addressed to:

Peter Dennis, 'Fieldhead', The Park, Mansfield, Nottinghamshire NG18 2AT,
UK, or email magie.h@ntlworld.com

The Publishers regret that they can enter into no correspondence upon
this matter.

EDITOR'S NOTE

For ease of comparison please refer to the following conversion table:

1 mile = 1.6km
1yd = 0.9m
1ft = 0.3m
1in = 2.54cm/25.4mm
1 gallon (US) = 3.8 liters
1 ton (US) = 907kg
1lb = 0.45kg

CONTENTS

INTRODUCTION

In June 1940, British Prime Minister Winston Churchill sent a memorandum to his chiefs of staff instructing them to establish Britain's first special-forces units: 'We have always set our faces against this idea but ... there ought to be at least 20,000 storm troops or "Leopards" drawn from existing units,' proclaimed Churchill, who was desperate for the British to hit back quickly at the Germans after the debacle of Dunkirk (quoted in Mortimer 2012: 127). The name 'Leopards' was subsequently ditched in favour of 'Commandos' – after the irregular Afrikaner units that had caused the British Army such trouble during the 2nd Anglo-Boer War (1899–1902) – and by November 1940 five units of Commandos had been formed and were undergoing training in Scotland.

One of the Commandos was 24-year-old Jeff Du Vivier, a Londoner who on the outbreak of war in 1939 was working as an assistant manager of a seaside hotel. Du Vivier enlisted in The London Scottish and was sent to Aberdeen, in the north of Scotland, for his basic training. By autumn 1940 he had tired of square-bashing, however, and longed for a more exciting life; when he heard about the Commandos he volunteered, one of hundreds of bored young soldiers who were posted to No. 11 (Scottish) Commando. 'There were over 700 volunteers all told but only 500 were required,' recalled Du Vivier, not long before his death in May 2010. 'So the commanding officer, Colonel [Dick] Pedder sorted us out by marching us from Galashiels to Ayr' (quoted in Mortimer 2004: 6).

The first 500 men to complete the 75-mile march across Scotland to the west coast town of Ayr were accepted into No. 11 (Scottish) Commando; the rest were returned to their unit. With their initiation over, No. 11 Commando moved north to the Isle of Arran and began to train in earnest alongside Nos 1, 6, 7 and 8 Commando. One of the No. 11 officers to pass selection was Capt Geoffrey Keyes, whose father was a Lord of the Admiralty and Director of Combined Operations. On 4 November 1940 Capt Keyes wrote to his family to tell them about life in Arran: 'I am in a beastly fit and hearty state, and we sail over the hills at great speed. We (that is the troop leaders) fire live rounds at our Soldiery now to impress upon them the horrors of war, and make them utilize the best cover. Most instructive and effective and brightens training no end'.

The Commandos were formed because Churchill envisaged deploying them in Occupied Europe, particularly France, but in January 1941 it was decided to send three of the five Commando units to the Middle East. The reason behind the decision was simple: the special forces had been raised to operate in conjunction with a large-scale offensive, but in 1941 the British Army was not in a position to launch such a strike in Europe. In the Middle East it was, however – particularly against Italy's long lines of communications along the North African coast and against the lightly defended islands in the Mediterranean.

On 1 February 1941, Nos 7, 8 and 11 Commando sailed for the Middle East, disembarking at Geneifa, Egypt, on 11 March and marching into a camp where they were inspected by Gen Sir Archibald Wavell, Commander-in-Chief

On becoming Prime Minister of Great Britain in June 1940, one of the first acts of Winston Churchill – seen here with the First Sea Lord, Admiral of the Fleet Sir Dudley Pound – was to instruct his chiefs of staff to establish Britain's first special-forces units. As a result the Commandos were born and one of the first volunteers was Geoffrey Keyes. (Cody Images)

Middle East. Wavell told the new arrivals that two further units of Commandos had been raised in the Middle East and would be added to Nos 7, 8 and 11 Commando to form 'Layforce' under the command of Col Robert Laycock. At this time No. 7 Commando became A Battalion, No. 8 Commando became B Battalion, No. 11 (Scottish) Commando became C Battalion, and two locally raised Commandos, Nos 50 and 52, merged to become D Battalion.

A Battalion was the first Layforce unit to see action, raiding the coastal port of Bardia, Cyrenaica, on 19 April with orders 'to harass the enemy's L. of C. [lines of communication] and inflict as much damage as possible on supplies and material'. 'We were pretty confident as we sailed towards Bardia,' recalled Albert Youngman of A Battalion. 'After months of training we thought we were finally going to get the chance to have a crack at the enemy.' Unfortunately, the British Commandos did just about everything but 'have a crack' at the Germans. Some detachments were landed at the wrong beach, while others came ashore way behind schedule and aborted their mission. 'It was a complete balls-up,' reflected Youngman. 'We were supposed to blow up this fuel dump but all we found were a heap of tyres. Then on the way back to the beach we ran into an enemy patrol and ended up fighting a rearguard.' B Battalion fared little better in the Middle East, the unit being split up and sent either to help in the evacuation of Crete or to reinforce the besieged garrison at Tobruk.

The 33 officers and 513 men of C Battalion, meanwhile, had been sent to the Mediterranean island of Cyprus at the end of April in anticipation of

Geoff Caton, seen here on the left during an SAS operation in the desert in 1942, was a member of No. 11 (Scottish) Commando and had fought alongside Geoffrey Keyes at Litani River, Syria, in June 1941. Caton would be killed during the Allied invasion of Sicily in July 1943.
(SAS Regimental Archive)

British Crusader tanks of 7th Armoured Division. In June 1941 the British launched Operation *Battleaxe*, the aim of which was to retake the territory lost to Rommel the previous spring. The offensive ended in failure, however, with the British tanks unable to burst through the strong German defensive positions, and consequently Archibald Wavell was replaced with Claude Auchinleck as Commander-in-Chief Middle East. (Cody Images)

a German invasion. A month later they had not had sight of the enemy and the men were growing restless – even self-possessed professional soldiers like Geoffrey Keyes (recently promoted to acting major), who complained in a letter home of the heat and the 'minor ailments' that had laid him low. Eventually, in June 1941, C Battalion was dispatched to Syria to participate in the offensive against the 30,000 Vichy French troops there who posed a threat to British interests in the Middle East. The Commandos helped secure a bridgehead for the Australian 21st Infantry Brigade at Litani River on 9 June, but casualties were high: 45 officers and men killed – including their commanding officer, Col Pedder – and another 84 wounded. Yet among the survivors there was a sense of quiet satisfaction at having been blooded in battle. A few weeks later in the House of Lords, Lord Croft, Under-Secretary of State for War, in describing the Syrian campaign, said: 'The Australians were greatly aided in crossing the Litani River by the landings of British infantry ... they were landed from ships of the Royal Navy, and took part in a very gallant action with decisive local tactical results, enabling the Australians to proceed'.

But by the time Lord Croft addressed the House of Lords, Layforce had ceased to exist. Keyes, promoted to acting lieutenant-colonel in the wake of Pedder's death, was told the news when visited by Laycock a few days after the action at Litani River. Despite his satisfaction at the achievements of C Battalion, Laycock informed Keyes that its men would either be returned to their original unit or used as replacements for undermanned regiments in North Africa.

This decision by Middle East Headquarters (MEHQ) had been prompted by two factors. First, Layforce had taken heavy casualties, not just at Litani River but also in Crete, where 70 per cent of the force had been killed or captured. There weren't enough men to replenish their diminished ranks, particularly as the British were launching a large offensive, Operation *Battleaxe* (15–17 June) against Generalleutnant Erwin Rommel's Deutsches Afrikakorps, the German force sent by Hitler to shore up his faltering Italian allies in the Middle East. Second, British intelligence reported that since Layforce had begun raiding targets along the Mediterranean coasts, Axis forces had strengthened their defences and were now largely immune to the type of raids envisaged by the British Commandos.

Blair Mayne, known to one and all as 'Paddy', was arguably the greatest special-forces soldier in the British Army during World War II, winning the DSO on four occasions for his exceptional gallantry. Originally a member of No. 11 (Scottish) Commando, Mayne resented the 'Bertie Wooster style' of Geoffrey Keyes and on one occasion manhandled the Englishman. (SAS Regimental Archive)

Keyes wrote to his father to express his disappointment at the news, saying: 'We are up against a wall of disbandment, just when we have proved ourselves. We are stuck here for a bit ... [and] we may go bust except for a few die-hards, one of which will be myself. I will try to keep the Hackle [No. 11 (Scottish) Commando] a power in the Middle East'. Throughout the summer Keyes strove to keep No. 11 (Scottish) Commando – as it had reverted to after the demise of Layforce – operational but in October 1941 he was instructed to join Eighth Army with what remained of his Commandos, approximately 110 men all told. Lt Tommy Macpherson, at this time Keyes' second-in-command, went with him, writing in his diary on 4 October: 'The men are still very good – particularly my own lads, though I say it myself! Some small jobs are promised and things look better, though several good officers and some not so good have gone off with David Stirling'.

The officers who had 'gone off' with Stirling had joined his new unit, provisionally entitled L Detachment of the Special Air Service (SAS) Brigade. Blair Mayne, Eoin McGonigal and Bill Fraser were three of the No. 11 (Scottish) Commando officers recruited by Stirling after his idea for a parachute-trained special-forces unit had been accepted in July 1941 by Gen Sir Claude Auchinleck, who had recently replaced Wavell as Commander-in-Chief Middle East. Another one of Keyes' soldiers now serving under Stirling was Jeff Du Vivier. 'We were just hanging around in the desert getting fed up,' he recalled. 'And then along came Stirling asking for volunteers. I was hooked on the idea from the beginning because it meant we were going to see some action' (quoted in Mortimer 2004: 14). For Maj Keyes and his 110 men the chances of seeing some action seemed as remote as ever in the second week of October 1941. Then on the 14th of that month there was a glimmer of hope. 'They [MEHQ] have something interesting on hand for us,' Keyes wrote and told his father.

ORIGINS

The first year of the war in North Africa was one of success for the British. General Rodolfo Graziani, the Italian commander-in-chief, had invaded Egypt in September 1940 but by early the following year his Tenth Army had been defeated by Britain's Western Desert Force (later known as Eighth Army). The final humiliation for Graziani came on 6 February 1941, at Beda Fomm, a small coastal town in south-western Cyrenaica (the eastern coastal regions of Libya), when the remnants of his army surrendered to the much smaller British 7th Armoured Division. The war in North Africa seemed to be drawing to a close.

But on the same day that the Italians suffered this abject defeat, a charismatic German general was in Berlin for an audience with Adolf Hitler. Rommel arrived in Tripoli on 12 February, followed two days later by the advance elements of his Deutsches Afrikakorps, which comprised

Generalmajor Rommel checks maps with officers of his 7. Panzer-Division in May 1940. As commander of the 'Ghost Division', Rommel faced the only major Allied counter-attack, at Arras, in which his forces inflicted significant losses among the British Matilda tanks that had initially caused havoc among the German defenders. His actions in the battle of France would form the basis for his formidable reputation as one of Nazi Germany's leading practitioners of armoured warfare. (NARA)

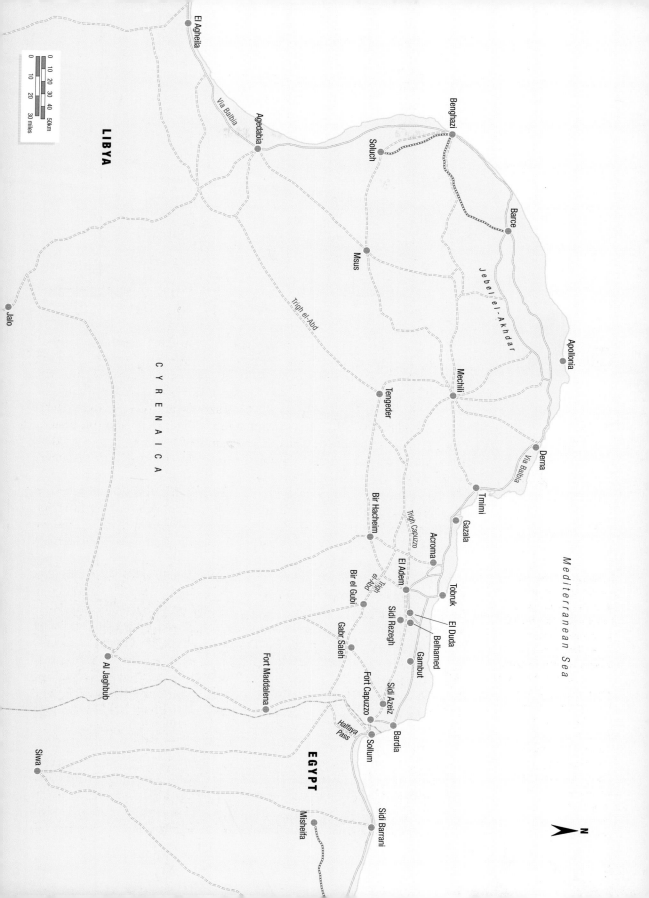

LIBYA

El Agheila

Via Balbia

Agedabia

Soluch

Benghazi

Barce

J e b e l   e l - A k h d a r

Msus

Apollonia

C Y R E N A I C A

Trigh el Abd

Mechili

Tengeder

Derna

Via Balbia

Bir Hacheim

Tmimi

Trigh Capuzzo

Gazala

Acroma

El Adem

Trigh el Abd

Tobruk

Bir el Gubi

Sidi Rezegh

El Duda

Belhamed

Gabr Saleh

Gambut

Fort Maddalena

Fort Capuzzo

Sidi Azeiz

Halfaya Pass

Bardia

Al Jaghbub

Sollum

EGYPT

Siwa

Sidi Barrani

Misheifa

Mediterranean Sea

Jalo

N

A PzKpfw I Ausf B in North Africa in April 1941. Two months after his arrival in North Africa, Rommel's Deutsches Afrikakorps had advanced 400 miles east, so that the Mediterranean port of Tobruk remained the sole British possession in Cyrenaica. (Cody Images)

5. leichte Division (a 'light' armoured formation that was later renamed 21. Panzer-Division) and 15. Panzer-Division. It took several weeks before the force was assembled in its entirety so Rommel improvised with the sort of cunning that would come to characterize his command in North Africa and earn him the sobriquet of the 'Desert Fox'. A squadron of dummy tanks was rushed up towards the front to fool the Allies into believing he had more armour than he actually did. The ruse worked, the British air reconnaissance unable to detect that the 'tanks' were in fact dummies mounted on Volkswagen motor cars.

Surprised by the Allies' passivity (7th Armoured Division had been withdrawn for a rest and refit following the emphatic British victory at Beda Fomm, and replaced with the inexperienced 2nd Armoured Division), Rommel kept advancing east and by late April 1941 the Deutsches Afrikakorps had pushed back the enemy as far as the Egyptian frontier. The Allies counter-attacked in June 1941 but Operation *Battleaxe* ended in failure, the British tanks unable to burst through the strong German defensive positions.

The defeat cost Gen Wavell his job as Commander-in-Chief Middle East; he was replaced by Gen Auchinleck, 'The Auk', one of whose mottos was 'Always be bold'. It was a philosophy espoused by Auchinleck's superior, Prime Minister Winston Churchill, who pressed his general to launch a new offensive against Rommel as quickly as possible. As reinforcements flooded into Egypt in the early autumn of 1941, Auchinleck began drawing up

the plans for Operation *Crusader* in November. Its overall aims were simple: to retake Cyrenaica and seize the Libyan airfields from the enemy, thereby enabling the Royal Air Force (RAF) to increase their supplies to Malta, the Mediterranean island that was of such strategic importance to the British.

To achieve these aims Auchinleck intended his XIII Corps to launch a frontal attack against the Axis forces holding the front line, while XXX Corps would swing round the flanks and annihilate Rommel's armoured force of 174 tanks, markedly inferior in number to the 710 tanks at Auchinleck's disposal. Meanwhile the besieged garrison at Tobruk, 70 miles behind the German front line, would break out and meet the units of XXX Corps as they advanced west across Cyrenaica. However, true to his motto, Auchinleck incorporated two other operations into *Crusader*, missions that were highly secretive and extremely audacious, and which would both coincide with the start of the offensive on 18 November.

The first involved the SAS who, after months of training, were desperate to embark on their first mission and prove their worth. Led by David Stirling, a 54-strong force would parachute into Cyrenaica on the night of 17 November, between the two vast opposing armies, and attack a string of Axis airfields at Gazala and Tmimi. The second mission was the 'something interesting' that Geoffrey Keyes had written to his father about in October, shortly before he and 58 of his Commandos departed to the Canal Zone to undergo a period of intensive training. Their task, ostensibly, was to raid Axis communication installations at Cirene, 250 miles west of Libya's border with Egypt, but they were also to attack a private villa in Beda Littoria (known to the Italians as Sidi Rafa) close by – which, according to British intelligence reports, was Rommel's headquarters. Assuming Rommel was at home, the Commandos were to kill him.

An aristocratic Scot, Lt David Stirling arrived in the Middle East in March 1941 as part of Layforce, the short-lived Commando unit led by Robert Laycock. From Layforce's failure, Stirling learned several valuable lessons upon which he drew when formulating his ideas for the guerrilla force that would become the Special Air Service. (Author's Collection)

GEOFFREY KEYES – THE ADMIRAL'S SON

Born in May 1917, the eldest son of Rear Admiral Sir Roger Keyes, Geoffrey grew up in the shadow of his illustrious father. Sir Roger – knighted and made a baron for his wartime services – was the daring leader of the Zeebrugge Raid in 1918, the death-or-glory attack on the German U-boat pens in the Belgian harbour that achieved more in propaganda than in actual material damage to the enemy submarines. In 1930 Sir Roger was promoted to admiral of the fleet and four years later, his naval career at its end, he entered politics, becoming Conservative Member of Parliament for North Portsmouth.

Geoffrey's childhood was privileged and exceptional. The family home welcomed such guests as Winston Churchill, the Duke and Duchess of York, and Lord and Lady Mountbatten, while Geoffrey was sent to Eton in 1931 to complete his education as an English gentleman. Though he tried hard to excel at team sports, Geoffrey suffered from poor eyesight and a bad back, and rugby proved beyond him. Polo and hunting were more his forte, and he exhibited an academic bent that won him a scholarship to the Royal Military College Sandhurst. In 1937 he was commissioned into The Royal Scots Greys, and the following year his regiment was posted to the Lebanon; Keyes was still there when war was declared with Germany on 3 September 1939.

From the outset Keyes was impatient to see action, preferably in some daring exploit similar to the Zeebrugge Raid that had made his father a celebrity. Geoffrey had proved to be an unexceptional soldier thus far, and his slight frame (he was 6ft 1in tall but weighed only 10 stone) didn't seem to be that of a born guerrilla fighter. Fortunately, he had his father. In July 1940, a month after Churchill had instructed his chiefs of staff to raise Britain's first special-forces units, Sir Roger was appointed the first Director of Combined Operations, tasked with organizing attacks on German targets by combined units of Royal Navy and Army forces.

Geoffrey Keyes was one of the first volunteers for the Commandos, joining No. 11 (Scottish) Commando in the summer of 1940. He wasn't a popular recruit, particularly among his fellow officers, who sensed nepotism at work in the way Keyes was promoted from lieutenant to acting major in the space of six months. 'Geoffrey was not everybody's cup of tea,' reflected Tommy Macpherson, who went with Keyes from No. 11 (Scottish) Commando to Layforce. 'He commanded a degree of respect, but again, he was not particularly liked' (quoted in Ross 2003: 51).

Even so, Keyes was brave, as he proved in winning a Military Cross with Layforce at Litani River. Yet this only added to his insufferable conceit in the eyes of some of his fellow officers, notably Lt Blair Mayne, who manhandled Keyes in the mess shortly after Litani River. 'I think he was hugely conscious of his heritage and the need to do well in a situation where he was not terribly well equipped to do well in the physical side of soldiering; he was not strong; he was tall and, you might say, weedy in build; he also was slightly more Bertie Wooster-style spoken than the rest of us' (quoted in Ross 2003: 52).

Lt-Col Geoffrey Keyes, son of the World War I admiral, used his famous father's influence to become an important figure within the Commandos. Not a guerrilla fighter by temperament, Keyes was, nonetheless, a brave man who – like his father – was awarded the Victoria Cross. (Cody Images)

ERWIN ROMMEL – THE DESERT FOX

In March 1941 Oberleutnant Heinz Schmidt, born in South Africa, was attached to Rommel's staff as his aide-de-camp on account of his knowledge of the continent. He later recalled his first meeting with the general, writing:

> His figure is compact and short ... he gives me a brief, powerful shake of the hand. Blue-grey eyes look steadily into mine. I notice that he has unusual humour-wrinkles slanting downward from above the corners of his eyes to the outer edges of his cheekbones. His mouth and chin are well-formed and strong, and reinforce my first impression of an energetic, vital personality. (Schmidt 1951: 11)

It was an impression that Rommel left on most people he met. Born in November 1891 in Württemberg in south-east Germany, Rommel had little military lineage. His father was a schoolteacher and his mother the daughter of a politician, and indeed Rommel dreamed as a schoolboy of becoming an engineer. Instead he joined the Army as an officer cadet in 1910, earning his commission in 1912 and serving initially as a recruitment officer in Infanterie-Regiment 'König Wilhelm I' (6. Württembergisches) Nr. 124.

When World War I erupted in August 1914, Rommel was sent to France within days, sustaining his first wound in September and winning an Iron Cross the following year. He later served in the Carpathians with distinction and by the time the war ended had earned a reputation as a brilliant officer of original mind. Against the backdrop of the emergence of Adolf Hitler and the Nazi Party in 1930s Germany, Rommel's military career flourished and in October 1935 he was promoted to Oberstleutnant (lieutenant-colonel) and appointed to the Kriegsakademie (War Academy) at Potsdam.

In September 1939, the month Germany went to war, Rommel was promoted to the rank of Generalmajor (major-general) and during the invasion of France and the Low Countries the following spring he commanded 7. Panzer-Division with stunning success. Deploying the initiative, originality and tenacity for which he was famous within Germany, Rommel's deployment of his force earned it the nickname

Posted to North Africa in February 1941 after the British had routed the Italians, by the time of the *Crusader* battles Rommel was a General der Panzertruppe commanding Panzergruppe Afrika. Here, amid other decorations, he sports the Pour le Mérite – Germany's highest award for valour – he won as an Oberleutnant commanding a company of mountain troops at Caporetto in 1917. (NARA)

'The Ghost Division' because of its habit of appearing suddenly. This was not just because of the speed with which the division moved through France, but also because Rommel frequently didn't reveal his whereabouts to the German High Command, whom he regarded as being ignorant of tank warfare.

Rommel's central role and immediate impact in the struggle for dominance in North Africa meant that as 1941 drew to a close, the British were desperate to counter his influence on the conduct of Axis operations in the theatre – and so Operation *Flipper* was conceived.

INITIAL STRATEGY

The identity of the person who proposed the attack on Rommel's HQ at Beda Littoria has never been officially revealed. After all, the British military didn't go in for assassinations, not officially at any rate. If there were any records pertaining to the operation they didn't survive the war; perhaps they were destroyed in late June 1942, when the Germans advanced so far east across the desert that British staff officers in MEHQ began burning documents in anticipation of the arrival of the Axis forces in Cairo.

However, the diary of Capt Tommy Macpherson implies it was Geoffrey Keyes himself whose idea it was to hunt down Rommel. On 4 October 1941, Macpherson wrote: 'A red letter day! Today Geoffrey found a great idea and we began to put it over – it will be a fight'. Later, Macpherson wrote to the Keyes family describing how Geoffrey had 'burst radiantly into our orderly room after a promising visit to headquarters and said "If we get this job, Tommy, it's one people will remember us by!"' In her biography of her brother, Elizabeth Keyes wrote in 1956 that it was Geoffrey who after 'much persuasion and many interviews … won over a reluctant and sceptical G.H.Q.', a view borne out by an account of the raid written subsequently by Col Robert Laycock, erstwhile commander of Layforce and in October 1941 the head of Middle East Commando. Laycock wrote:

> The original plan, formulated several weeks in advance at 8 A.H.Q. [Advanced Headquarters was an organization specializing in rescuing prisoners of war] included orders for attacks on various separate objectives. Although the whole operation was considered to be of a somewhat desperate nature it was obvious that certain tasks were more dangerous than others. Colonel K[eyes] was present at all the meetings and assisted in the planning, deliberately selected for himself from the outset the command of the det.[ail] detached to attack what was undoubtedly the most hazardous of these objectives – the residence and H.Q. of the General Officer Commanding the German forces in North Africa.

Col Robert Laycock, seen here inspecting Special Service troops later in the war, was the commander of the ill-fated Layforce, the Commando unit sent to the Middle East in early 1941. Laycock accompanied the raiders on the mission to 'get Rommel' and would be one of only three survivors to return. (Cody Images)

> When the plan was submitted to me as Comdr of the M.E. Commandos, I gave it my considered opinion that the chances of being evacuated after the operation were very slender and that the attack on Gen. R.'s house in particular appeared to be desperate in the extreme. This attack even if initially successful, meant almost certain death for those who took part in it. I made these comments in the presence of Col. Keyes who begged me not to repeat them lest the operation be cancelled. (WO 218/171)

Despite the misgivings he later claimed to have harboured over the raid, Laycock authorized the plan, and Keyes and his 58 men began training for the operation off a stretch of coastline near Alexandria in Egypt. Using rubber dinghies and folboats (folding kayaks), the Commandos practised beach landings at night. Laycock, meanwhile, instructed Capt John Haselden to lead a small reconnaissance party overland to verify the intelligence concerning Rommel's headquarters at Beda Littoria. Again, because of the lack of extant records about the operation, it is impossible to say from where the information first came. It was probably a British spy – a trusted one, evidently, as MEHQ appeared quite convinced that Rommel's HQ was at Beda Littoria.

Haselden was a fascinating individual, the nearest the British came in World War II to producing another 'Lawrence of Arabia'. Born in 1903 at Ramleh near Alexandria, Egypt, Haselden married the beautiful Nadia Ida Marie Szymonski-Lubicz in Alexandria in 1931 and had a good job as a cotton merchant while his brother held a position in Egypt with Barclays Bank. The birth of his son completed the idyll but then shortly before

This photo of SBS personnel is believed to have been taken in early 1941, not long after the unit's establishment by Capt Roger Courtney. The three soldiers are in a collapsible kayak – better known as a folboat. (Author's Collection)

the war Haselden's wife was killed in an automobile accident. The outbreak of war offered Haselden an outlet for his grief, and his fluency in Arabic, French and Italian made him appealing to MEHQ, who appointed him Western Desert Liaison Officer at Eighth Army HQ, working closely together with the Long Range Desert Group (LRDG). In particular, Haselden was instructed to obtain information from friendly Arabs in the region. A MEHQ report described Haselden as 'a very remarkable man with a great influence over the Desert Arabs' (quoted in PRO 2001: 419).

On 10 October Haselden was landed by the submarine *Torbay* at Chescem el-Kelb, a small beach on the coast of Cyrenaica approximately 18 miles from Beda Littoria, on which it was planned to land the raiding party the following month. Haselden, disguised as a local and accompanied by an Arab companion, moved inland towards the village of Slonta, 12 miles south of Beda Littoria. The terrain the pair had to traverse was wild and rugged, known locally as the *Jebel el-Akhdar* ('Green Mountain'). In reality, however, for most of the year the relentless sun bleached the grass white – and anyway it was stripped down to the red rock underneath by grazing goats and sheep. As for the 'mountain', this was in fact an escarpment of two tiers with a sloping shelf in between and a flat surface on the top.

The land rose approximately 1,000ft between the first tier and the second, with the step in between fractured with myriad gullies and *wadis* (dry riverbeds) covered in scrubland. In the winter months the desert storms could turn these *wadis* into raging torrents. Further inland, on the south side of the mountain, the terrain was flatter and more arid, and there were ancient tombs and columns from the Greek colony that had flourished in Cirene for centuries before the Romans arrived in 100 BC.

Once at Slonta, Haselden and his Arab companion made contact with the village elder, Hussein Taher, a Senussi tribesman working for the Allies against the hated Italians. For nearly 20 years the Senussi had been engaged in a vicious war against the troops of Benito Mussolini, with the Italian fascist dictator determined to bring the Arabs to heel. Atrocities were frequent as the Italians struggled to contain the rebellious Senussi, and eventually

Opposite: Beda Littoria and environs, 1941.

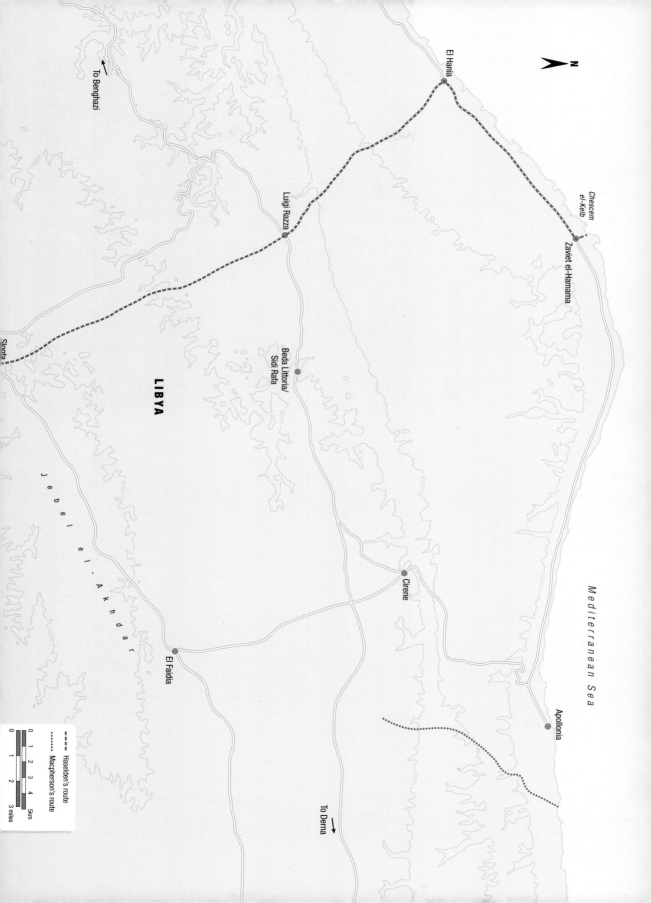

N

To Benghazi

El Hania

Chescem
el-Kelb

Zaviet el-Hamama

Luigi Razza

Beda Littoria/
Sidi Rafa

LIBYA

Slonta

J e b e l   e l - A k h d a r

Cirene

Mediterranean Sea

El Faidia

Apollonia

To Derna

Haselden's route
Macpherson's route

0   1   2   3   4   5km
0   1   2   3 miles

The fascist leader of Italy, Benito Mussolini, had ordered the invasion of Libya in the 1920s but despite the Italians' overwhelming superiority in manpower and weaponry, they struggled to bring the Senussi tribesmen under control. As a result the Senussi proved useful allies to the British during the war in North Africa. (Cody Images)

Mussolini had been compelled to construct a barbed-wire fence along the entire length of his eastern frontier.

Whether the information concerning Rommel's headquarters at Beda Littoria came from Senussi sources is unknown. But after a good night's rest and plenty of food, Haselden and his guide embarked on a reconnaissance of the area accompanied by friendly tribesmen and gathered intelligence about German and Italian troop deployments in the neighbourhood. Once his reconnaissance was complete, Haselden made for his rendezvous with an LRDG patrol led by Capt Jake Easonsmith. He arrived to discover the LRDG had an Italian prisoner, a member of the 'Trieste' Motorized Division captured on the way to Mechili, who talked freely as the patrol made its way to the desert hideout at Siwa Oasis. From there Haselden travelled on to Alexandria, arriving on 27 October to give Keyes and Laycock a thorough briefing on all he had learned.

According to the Arabs there was no doubt Rommel's headquarters was located half a mile west of the village of Beda Littoria and surrounded by a cypress grove. His offices were in the former prefecture – and Arab agents had even described to Haselden the plates on the doors – but the German general slept in a whitewashed villa at the far end of the village.

While Haselden had been reconnoitring the territory around Beda Littoria, Tommy Macpherson had been inserted east of the village to carry out a similar reconnaissance between Apollonia, on the coast, and Cirene, headquarters of the Italian forces. Leaving Alexandria in the submarine

HMS *Talisman*, Macpherson paddled ashore at Apollonia with a Glaswegian corporal called Evans on the night of 26 October, and was accompanied by two officers from the Special Boat Section (SBS). The quartet negotiated the first tier of the escarpment – which consisted of a proliferation of rocks and thorns in similar quantities – and surveyed a suitable place on the step for the raiding party to rendezvous with its guide the following month.

Macpherson, Evans and the two SBS officers retraced their steps to the beach, found their folboats and paddled out towards the rendezvous, seven minutes ahead of schedule. There was no submarine, however (it later transpired they were waiting off the wrong beach), and an increasingly rough swell forced them back towards land, wrecking their kayaks and leaving them no choice but to strike out on foot for the besieged British garrison at Tobruk. For more than a week the four men made their way east, moving mostly at night and stealing food and water from German mobile workshops whenever they could. Then, on the night of 3 November, they were approaching the port of Derna when 'on an apparently empty side road we walked straight into the middle of some thirty men of a bicycle patrol' (quoted in Keyes 1956: 202). The four soldiers were taken to Derna and from there ferried across the Mediterranean to an Italian prisoner-of-war camp. The capture of Macpherson was a bitter blow for Keyes, but he determined to press on with the attack despite the loss of his second-in-command and the misgivings of Col Laycock.

3 NOVEMBER 1941

Macpherson captured during reconnaissance mission

One of the earliest-known photographs of the SBS, taken in the Middle East in 1941. Many of these men were killed or captured on operations, leading to the SBS's incorporation into the SAS the following year. (Author's Collection)

THE LONG RANGE DESERT GROUP

The LRDG was the brainchild of Ralph Bagnold, a veteran of World War I and a noted North African desert explorer of the late 1920s and early 1930s. In June 1940 Capt Bagnold submitted an idea for a desert reconnaissance force to Gen Wavell, who authorized Bagnold to establish his unit, provisionally called the Long Range Patrol. As Bagnold wrote later, there would be three patrols, 'every vehicle of which, with a crew of three and a machine gun, was to carry its own supplies of food and water for 3 weeks, and its own petrol for 2500 miles of travel across average soft desert surface – equivalent in petrol consumption to some 2400 miles of road' (quoted in Mortimer 2012: 162). Travelling in American Chevrolet 30-cwt trucks purchased from the Egyptian Army or from vehicle dealers in Cairo, and wearing Arab headdresses and leather sandals rather than British Army-issue leather boots and service-dress caps, the Long Range Patrol soon became the Long Range Desert Group.

For officers, Bagnold recruited some of his fellow explorers such as Bill Kennedy Shaw and Pat Clayton, while the men were enlisted predominantly from the New Zealand and Rhodesian forces because, in Bagnold's view, the average British soldier was 'apt to be wasteful' while the average 'Colonial' soldier was 'alert, intelligent and possessed of a sense of responsibility' (quoted in Mortimer 2012: 163).

In August 1940 the LRDG embarked on its first mission, led by Pat Clayton, a reconnaissance of the Jalo–Kufra track used by the Italians in Benghazi to resupply their garrisons at Kufra and Uweinat. Having driven east into Libya, Clayton's two-vehicle patrol watched the track for three days but observed no enemy vehicles. But it wasn't a wasted expedition. Having penetrated 600 miles from his base, Clayton returned to Egypt with two important details. First, enemy aircraft rarely detected sand-coloured vehicles in the desert as long as they were stationary. Second, he had discovered a route that crossed first the Egyptian Sand Sea and then, once inside Libya, the Kalanhso Sand Sea. The two seas were in fact connected further north to form, as Bagnold later described, 'an irregular horseshoe' shape in the south (quoted in Mortimer 2012: 164). Clayton had pioneered a route across the two Sand Seas that would become the point of entry into Libya for future LRDG patrols.

By December 1940 the LRDG was proving so invaluable as a reconnaissance force that it was expanded, a new patrol being formed from the Guards regiments. The following year it began working with David Stirling's SAS, providing the ears and the eyes to the guerrilla unit while they were the muscle. Though they jokingly referred to the LRDG as the Long Range Taxi Group – they would be driven to and from targets by the LRDG – the men of the SAS had enormous respect for the LRDG's skills. So, too, did Gen Wavell, who in a dispatch at the end of 1941 declared: 'Their journeys across vast regions of unexplored desert have entailed the crossing of physical obstacles and the endurance of extreme temperatures, both of which a year ago would have been deemed impossible. Their exploits have been achieved only by careful organisation and a very high standard of enterprise, discipline, mechanical maintenance and desert navigation' (quoted in Mortimer 2012: 176).

The LRDG were ingenious in their modes of transport. Though they began by using American Chevrolet 30-cwt trucks, they were apt to improvise, as seen here in this photo. It shows a Ford V-8 staff car cut down to resemble a German staff car. It was later used by SAS commander David Stirling. (SAS Regimental Museum)

THE PLAN

The operation takes shape

The operation was given the codename *Flipper*, and Laycock and Keyes drew up the plan at AHQ in the first week of November. The party was divided into four detachments: No. 1 party, comprising Lt-Col Keyes with two officers and 22 other ranks, on HMS *Torbay*; No. 2 party, comprising Lt D. Sutherland with 12 other ranks, on HMS *Talisman*; No. 3 party, comprising Lt Chevalier with 11 other ranks, also on *Talisman*; and HQ party, comprising Col Laycock with two other ranks and a medical orderly, on *Torbay*. There were also two Senussi guides for Nos 1 and 2 parties, and a folboat party of two officers and two other ranks.

The wreckage of a British Matilda tank following fierce fighting during Operation *Crusader* in November 1941, the aim of which was to retake the eastern coastal regions of Cyrenaica. To complement the operation, Gen Auchinleck authorized two special-forces raids: Keyes' operation and the first SAS mission, led by David Stirling. (Cody Images)

The one curiosity of the operational plan for *Flipper* that has never been adequately explained was the presence of Col Laycock, seen here in 1943 as a major-general. Why would the commander of the Middle East Commando imperil himself by going on such a risky operation, even if he was to remain on the landing beach with the HQ party as an 'observer'? Was it, in the event of Rommel being captured, to relieve the young Geoffrey Keyes of the emotional pressure of deciding the fate of the German general? In other words, had Laycock nominated himself as Rommel's actual assassin? (IWM TR 1425)

Four objectives were outlined. These were: (No. 1 party) Rommel's house and the German HQ, believed to be at Beda Littoria; (No. 2 party) the Italian HQ at Cirene; (No. 3 party) the Italian Intelligence Centre at Apollonia; (HQ party) to act as a report centre and rear link. In addition to the tasks specified in the 'Operation Order and Plan', Haselden would destroy the telephone and telegraph communications on the road from Lamluda to El Faidia.

If all went according to plan, then the four raiding parties were to lie up during 15 November and move to other concealed lie-up locations halfway to their targets during the night of 15/16 November. They would lie up the following day, move closer to the targets during the night of the 16/17th, and observe the objectives during the daylight hours of 17 November. The simultaneous attacks would then be launched at 2359hrs on 17 November, a few hours before Operation *Crusader* commenced.

Once the raiders had carried out their objectives, they would head back to the landing beach at Chescem el-Kelb, where the submarines would be waiting to collect them from the fourth to the sixth nights after landing. *Torbay* would be off Chescem el-Kelb and *Talisman* 3 miles to the west. The two vessels were both T-submarines, launched in early 1940, and capable of a maximum speed of 9 knots submerged. Skipper of *Torbay* was Lt-Cdr Anthony 'Crap' Miers, a controversial figure who had been reprimanded by the Royal Navy after admitting in an official report on the sinking of an enemy ship that he had surfaced and 'with the Lewis gun accounted for the soldiers in the rubber raft to prevent them from regaining their ship' (Ziogaite et al. 1999). Even so, Miers was recognized as being a brilliant commander who had dispatched a dozen enemy vessels since arriving in the Mediterranean; he would be awarded the Victoria Cross in March 1942 for a daring attack against German shipping in the South Corfu Channel.

Training and preparation

In Alexandria, the training intensified, with Keyes and his men continuing to practise their seafaring skills from the depot ship HMS *Medway*. 'The hardest bit by far was finding the submarine again when we paddled back out to sea [in rubber dinghies],' recalled Sgt Cyril Feebery, a member of the SBS's folboat section. 'You had to make allowances for those same currents on the Folboat. Then there was the wind. Inflatable dinghies skid about like bubbles in the lightest breeze even with large men aboard' (Feebery 2008: 37).

Keyes, meanwhile, was finalizing his raiding party. Having decided to take one of his two Commando troops (approximately 53 men), he then enlisted two Senussi guides from the Libyan Arab Force, men handpicked by Capt Haselden, as well as an interpreter – Cpl Abshalom Drori, a Palestinian Commando. Keyes wasn't at all what Drori was expecting when he arrived in Alexandria. 'I was surprised to encounter a tall young man in shorts who smiled at me, offered me a seat and asked me some questions about my abilities as a linguist,' recalled Drori. Once he was accepted as the unit's interpreter, Drori took the chance to observe the Commandos in the final stages of their training and noted that 'Keyes never gave an order, he just used to talk to the men, and they always fulfilled his instructions as a matter of course as if they were doing it on their own account'.

Among the officers selected for the mission by Keyes was Capt Robin Campbell, a 29-year-old with an artistic bent whose father, Sir Ronald, was the British Ambassador to Portugal, having fulfilled a similar function in France from 1939 to 1940. Campbell had been a member of Layforce, but since its disbandment had worked at a desk job in Cairo; Keyes chose him not because of his soldiering skills, but because he was fluent in German. Similarly inexperienced in Commando warfare was Lt Roy Cooke of The Queen's Own Royal West Kent Regiment, who found that though Keyes was the younger man 'he had the personality to leave me feeling rather like a schoolboy does to his First Fifteen Captain'.

At midday on 10 November Keyes paraded his men and informed them they would be sailing for their destination in two hours' time. None of them yet knew where or what their intended objective would be. In the two hours prior to embarkation

The SBS camp at Athlit, on the coast approximately 8 miles south of Haifa in Palestine, was an ideal location for the Commandos. Here the likes of David Sutherland and Tommy Langton had helped to turn the unit into one of the deadliest of all World War II special forces. (SAS Regimental Archive)

Graham Rose (left) and Jimmy Storie, two original members of the SAS, prepare for another mission deep behind enemy lines in 1942. Like Keyes and Campbell, most of the early SAS had served in Layforce before its disbandment in the summer of 1941. (SAS Regimental Association)

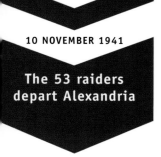

10 NOVEMBER 1941

The 53 raiders depart Alexandria

Keyes made two decisions that illustrated his naivety about the nature of the mission and what it would entail. One of his men, L/Cpl Frank Varney, after suffering from sore feet for a number of days, had gone to see the medical orderly, an ex-circus performer who thought neat iodine cured most ailments. The ointment stripped the skin from Varney's feet and prompted Keyes to remove him from the raiding party. Varney begged to be taken, however, telling Keyes that he wouldn't be 'able to look the other chaps in the face if I didn't go as it would look as if the injury was purposely done'. Keyes relented, and Varney and his painful feet boarded the submarine. So, too, did another brave soldier who convinced Keyes that his dysentery was of the mild strain and would soon disappear.

The raiders depart

The raiders were two hours late in embarking and it wasn't until 1600hrs that Lt-Col Keyes, Capt Campbell and Lt Cooke, together with 25 other ranks (ORs), boarded HMS *Torbay*. The other half of the raiding party, including Col Laycock, Capt Ian Glennie – who had fought with No. 11 (Scottish) Commando at Litani River – and Lt Sutherland, stowed themselves on HMS *Talisman*, which was commanded by Capt Michael Willmott. Among the men were six soldiers from the SBS – Lt Ken 'Tramp' Allot, Sgt Cyril Feebery, Lt Bob Ingles, Lt Tommy Langton, Cpl Clive Severn and a sixth man whose identity is not known. Their role in the operation was to paddle ashore in their folboats and ensure the coast was clear prior to the main landing.

Sutherland, who had just turned 21, knew Keyes from Eton and was another of the well-connected young Commando officers who found themselves at a loose end in the Middle East in the summer of 1941. The pair had been in the same house at Eton and though Keyes was Sutherland's senior by three years they 'used to sit around comfortably in the Cecil Hotel on the Corniche in Alexandria and wait for news' (Sutherland 1998: 46). In between whisky and sodas at the Cecil Hotel, Sutherland had used his time in the Middle East wisely, taking a demolition course at Geneifa and becoming an accomplished kayaker. It was in return for instructing Keyes' Commandos in demolition techniques that Sutherland had been accepted onto the raiding party.

Just a few hours into the voyage, however, Sutherland regretted his role in the operation. 'It was like Dante's inferno,' he recalled of the conditions inside *Talisman*. 'We were unbelievably crowded and hot, bodies lying everywhere' (Sutherland 1998: 47). In addition to the raiders, each submarine also held arms and ammunition, rations, seven rubber dinghies and two folboats. Men slept where they could, some on the wardroom floor and others squeezed into the torpedo tubes. The only relief from the claustrophobia was at night when the submarines surfaced and the soldiers gulped in the fresh air.

Two days out from Alexandria, Keyes and Laycock revealed the exact nature of the operation to the men. Their mission, explained Keyes, was 'to get Rommel'. With the men fully briefed, Keyes suggested they might want to write to their families, just in case. He then sat down and composed two letters, the first to the woman he loved, who had recently informed him she was marrying another man. Having congratulated the woman on her impending marriage, Keyes wrote:

> I am on my way to do more dirty work at the Crossroads. It is by no means an easy task, it is my show, my men, and my responsibility. The chances of getting away with it are moderately good, but if you get this letter, it means I have made a bit of a bog, and not got back.

Lt David Sutherland, seen here at his wedding in 1946, had been in the same house as Geoffrey Keyes at Eton, and the pair were reunited in the Middle East. Sutherland was one of the raiders on *Talisman* who would be unable to land because of the stormy conditions. (Author's Collection)

LRDG and SAS personnel pose for a photograph at one of their desert hideouts deep behind enemy lines. It was from one of these that Capt John Haselden set out to meet the raiding party at the beach. (SAS Regimental Museum)

To his family Keyes wrote in a similar vein, initially, at least, telling them: 'If this thing is a success, whether I get bagged [captured] or not, it will help the cause.' But then he let slip his apprehension when he wrote: 'It may be perfectly alright, in which case this won't be posted, but I am not happy about the future really.'

Towards the beach

As *Torbay* and *Talisman* sailed towards the beach at Chescem el-Kelb, Capt Haselden was once more making his way towards the village of Slonta and a rendezvous with Hussein Taher, the tribal elder. Haselden had set out with the LRDG from Siwa Oasis on 7 November; after the LRDG dropped him at the southern end of the *wadi* Heleigma, he continued on foot to Slonta, arriving on the night of 13 November. 'He asked me to help him to get two men to go with him,' said Hussein Taher, recalling Haselden's arrival at his house. The British officer also requested a horse, explaining it was for an 'important mission'. 'When dawn came I had everything needed and he left'. Haselden rode north towards the landing beach and sat down to await the arrival of the raiders.

Torbay and *Talisman* arrived off the coast of Cyrenaica on the evening of 14 November and submerged for a periscope reconnaissance of the landing beach at Chescem el-Kelb. In Lt-Cdr Miers' view the weather was 'ideal for carrying out the intended operations, but owing to overriding military considerations the opportunity was not accepted' (quoted in PRO 2001: 288). Instead, the two vessels remained at sea during the night and on the morning of 15 November an Italian Caproni Ca.309 *Ghibli* aircraft was spotted flying low over the coast in the direction of the *Talisman* and *Torbay*. The submarines dived to avoid detection and in doing so only partially received a signal. According to Miers the garbled signal was a cause of concern, with Keyes anxious that it might have been an order to abort the operation, but when the signal was sent a second time it proved to be confirmation of the landing date.

The weather deteriorated throughout the day on 15 November, with a strong wind agitating the sea and a driving wind reducing visibility. Nevertheless, Miers decided 'in view of the importance of the operation, the eagerness of the military to be landed and the improbability of the weather improving in the next few days, to effect the disembarkation in the prevailing conditions' (quoted in PRO 2001: 288). In fact, *Torbay's* log noted that the wind was Force 4 at midnight, increasing gradually to Force 7.

Torbay closed the beach at 1900hrs as the SBS soldiers scanned the shore through the rain. 'There was one moment none of us will ever forget. It was as we were closing the beach in *Torbay*,' recalled Lt Tommy Langton. Langton was a special-forces veteran, an officer in the Irish Guards who had joined No. 8 Commando before it was subsumed into Layforce. A double rowing blue for Cambridge in the late 1930s, Langton was, recalled David Sutherland, 'one of the most powerful swimmers I have ever seen' (Sutherland 1998: 40). Langton continued:

The beach at Chescem el-Kelb, where the raiders landed on the night of 15 November. The sea conditions were so bad that HMS *Talisman* would be unable to land 18 of its Commandos, leaving Keyes with only 36 men to carry out his mission. (Photograph courtesy Steve Hamilton – Western Desert Battlefield Tours)

We were on the forward casing of the submarine, blowing up the dinghies and generally preparing. We could just see the dark coast line ahead. We had been told that Haselden would be there to meet us, but I think no one really believed that he would. He had left Cairo quite three weeks before, and during the interval there had been several changes of plan... When the darkness was suddenly stabbed by his torch, making

the looked for signal, there was a gasp of amazement and relief from everyone – in other circumstances it would undoubtedly have been a spontaneous cheer. (www.combinedops.com)

14 NOVEMBER 1941
EVENING

The submarines arrive off Chescem-el-Kelb

15 NOVEMBER 1941
EVENING

Raiders from *Torbay* paddle ashore

The landing commences

Once Miers had confirmed the signal, at 1956hrs Lt Ingles and Cpl Severn launched their folboat into a heavy swell and began paddling towards the beach. Having contacted Haselden on the beach, Ingles and Severn waited for the first of the Commandos to paddle ashore. However, by now *Torbay* was experiencing difficulty in manoeuvring in the rough seas. Also finding the conditions a challenge were the raiders, who had been busy passing up the rubber dinghies through the forward hatch and inflating them on the deck of the submarine with a foot pump. A solitary wire ran fore and aft on *Torbay* 'and the men, who were lined up two by two on the forward casing, had to hold on to this with one hand and prevent their dinghies sliding off the deck with the other'.

Initially all went well, but when *Torbay* trimmed down in readiness for the launch of the dinghies a large wave crashed over the casing, sweeping the four aftermost rubber boats into the sea along with Cpl Spike Hughes, a 40-year-old former postman from London. 'I can't swim much!' cried Hughes, as he disappeared underneath the black foam of the Mediterranean. Luckily for Hughes, at the moment the wave hit, he had just finished inflating his two Mae West life jackets. 'I grabbed hold of a dinghy, clambered in, caught another one and tied the two together and felt quite safe,' recounted Hughes. 'One dinghy is difficult enough to handle, two together are hopeless. I could see the sub, but the more I paddled the further I seemed to drift away. After what seemed an hour, but which may have been only a few minutes, the current took me near the sub. I called out and they threw me a rope'. Hughes had indeed been in the water for a short time, but by the time he had been rescued, and the dinghies recovered, *Torbay* was obliged 'to go West for two miles to get back to her previous position' (PRO 2001: 288).

Concerned by the unexplained delay, Ingles and Severn had paddled back from the beach, arriving at *Torbay* at 2155hrs, just as the raiders tried once more to launch their rubber dinghies into the treacherous seas. The first seven dinghies were launched but then an eastward drift again disrupted the disembarkation, so that it wasn't until 2240hrs that launching was resumed. Miers was becoming agitated by the delays, writing in his report that 'perhaps the less well trained soldiers were being launched – at any rate boats capsized again and again, and in several cases the gear (boots, blankets, shirt and rations wrapped up in an anti-gas cape) was lost overboard' (PRO 2001: 289). The gear was sealed in a watertight container that was attached to the underside of the rubber dinghy.

The SBS party was also suffering at the hands of the sea, one wave smashing Ingles' unoccupied folboat against the side of the submarine and breaking it in two. To counter the conditions, Miers manoeuvred his submarine close to the spit at the end of the bay so that *Torbay* was in a slight lee by midnight.

The last dinghy to be launched caused the most problems, capsizing three times before finally it got clean away at 0030hrs on 16 November, with the two Commandos paddling for the shore undaunted. It had been a trying few hours for all concerned, and even an experienced and pugnacious commander such as Miers found the experience testing. He was full of praise for his submariners, as he was for the Commandos, writing:

> Those of the crew who took part received a very severe buffeting while handling the boats alongside in the swell and nearly all of them were completely exhausted at the finish. No less splendid was the spirit of the soldiers under strange and even frightening conditions. They were quite undaunted by the setbacks experienced, and remained quietly determined to get on with the job. (PRO 2001: 289)

The raiders regroup

Once ashore, Keyes and his Commandos were led by Haselden to one of a scattering of ruined houses a couple of hundred yards from the beach, where they stripped off their wet clothes and warmed themselves round a fire, a mug of hot tea in each man's hands. A few then got their heads down for a short rest while others waited to greet the second party from *Talisman*. Miers signalled to *Talisman* at 0035hrs that the operation was completed before *Torbay* put out to sea to transmit a message from Haselden to Eighth Army and to report the successful completion of the first raiding party to the wireless station in Rosyth, Scotland.

The message from *Torbay* was gratefully received on board *Talisman*, where Laycock had been mystified by the delay. Becoming ever more fretful

After Capt John Haselden guided the raiding party ashore on the night of 15 November the bedraggled Commandos huddled round a campfire inside one of the ruined houses to the east of the beach. This photograph shows the renovated houses at Chescem el-Kelb in 2012. (Photograph courtesy Steve Hamilton – Western Desert Battlefield Tours)

as the evening wore on, Laycock ordered Lt John 'Farmer' Pryor of the SBS to get in his folboat and find out what was the matter. Pryor was pretty sure he could make out *Torbay*'s conning tower as he and his No. 2, Cpl John Brittlebank of the Royal Artillery, climbed into their kayak. 'When it came to going up and down from sea-level, damned if I could find the *Torbay*,' recalled Pryor. 'And after ten minutes or so fruitless paddle [*sic*] returned to the *Talisman* and said I couldn't find her.' Capt Willmott, skipper of *Talisman*, pointed his submarine straight at *Torbay* and told Pryor all he had to do now was paddle in a straight line. 'I did so but still didn't find her,' recalled the SBS officer. 'However I came across a rubber dinghy with two Glaswegians in it, who said that they were the last dinghy of the *Torbay* and they "hoped to get ashore some time" ... I went back to Captain Willmott and told him this'.

Minutes after the return of Pryor from his abortive attempt to establish contact with *Torbay*, Willmott received the signal from Miers informing him that his half of the raiding party had been landed successfully. Willmott immediately instructed Pryor to paddle to shore and stand on the beach with a flashlight and signal the letter 'C', whereupon the Commandos would launch their dinghies. 'I set off to do this,' recalled Pryor:

> The *Torbay* party by this time had met Haselden and the venerable Arab he had with him. As there were no Italians about they had lit a fire in a ruined house on the beach, round which the men were trying to dry themselves. Seeing the fire I paddled for it, and it drew me too far to the east. Before I could stop we were capsized in surf on the rocks. We hung on to the canoe [*sic*], as we didn't want to have the wreckage about, and managed to struggle on to the rocks, but kept being sucked off by the undertow and knocked over by the waves.

Abandoning the kayak on the advice of Brittlebank, Pryor and his companion swam into a little rectangular bay, staggering ashore close to where the men of *Torbay* were warming themselves round the campfire. Pryor told Brittlebank to get dry and then 'stood miserably cold flashing C–C–C for a long time. I found I was slightly less cold without my shirt and stood naked C–C–Cing'. Geoffrey Keyes and Roy Cooke joined the shivering spectacle on the beach and laughed at Pryor's plight.

Keyes' high spirits weren't matched on board *Talisman*, where Capt Willmott was confronted with an awkward decision. The length of time it had taken the Commandos from *Torbay* to land had eaten considerably into his launch window; now he had just 3½ hours to get his 25 raiders safely onto the beach. On the plus side, however, the wind had dropped and the sea was less troublesome. At 0137hrs *Talisman* began to close on the beach, but eight minutes later, just as the first dinghy was about to be launched, 'the ground swell increased without warning' as the vessel touched the ocean floor. A wave reared up over the submarine, crashing down on the casing and sweeping away seven of the eight boats and 11 men.

Moments before, David Sutherland and Robert Laycock had been sitting in their dinghies discussing the stars above them. 'We were just talking about the Pole Star and its importance in navigation when the *Talisman* ran aground on the beach,' remembered Sutherland. 'A green sea swept over the forecasing from behind us and I saw Robert Laycock's jaw tighten as he and his companion were hurled headlong into the boiling water. Luckily I had both arms over the steel jumper wire that runs along the forecasing' (Sutherland 1998: 48).

To escape the swell Willmott was forced to go astern into deeper water and dispatch one of the SBS's folboats to help in the rescue of the men. The folboat, containing Ken Allott, was smashed by the vindictive sea as it was being launched, leaving Willmott with no option but to order Sutherland 'to throw in the remaining boats clear of the submarine and get his men to jump in after them. The men very pluckily carried out this order, but only one boat got away the right way up with the men on board' (PRO 2001: 289). For the next two hours *Talisman* plucked men and dinghies from the sea, but by the time the search-and-rescue mission was complete it was 0400hrs and the moon was up. In addition, one of the submarine's hydroplanes had been damaged and its batteries needed recharging. Only ten men had been launched from the *Talisman*, among them Laycock, leaving 18 raiders still on board the submarine – one Commando, L/Cpl Peter Barrand of the London Rifle Brigade, drowned during the attempted landings, despite the fact he had been wearing two Mae Wests when his body washed ashore.

Once Laycock reached the beach he signalled to *Talisman* with an electric torch, informing Willmott they would hide the boats while requesting they collect those ones still adrift. Astonishingly, Keyes hadn't brought any skilled signallers with him, because all the Commandos trained in this art had been transferred to other regiments following the disbandment of Layforce. He had had time, nevertheless, to recruit a proficient signaller for the mission but instead relied on Laycock's slipshod skills. Though he had taken a crash course in signalling, the colonel's signals were often misunderstood, a state of affairs not helped by the fact he had only a standard torch with no signalling key.

While Haselden's Arab companion led the Commandos to a cave where the rubber dinghies were stowed, the raiders swept the beach of all incriminating evidence of their presence. For an hour or so before dawn, Keyes paced the beach in the hope of spotting some stragglers from *Talisman* (which had now submerged and was recharging its battery). But he saw none, and eventually Robin Campbell persuaded his commanding officer to return to the campfire.

'Just before first light, Keyes gave the order to assemble the stores and personal kit and to follow him inland to a wadi [approximately 1 mile inland], which he had previously selected from the map as a good place to lie up in during the following day,' recalled Campbell, who said Pryor and Brittlebank were detailed to remain on the beach. 'The men were dispersed in various old ruined houses and caves all round the bed of the little dry stream, where they huddled together and slept – as cold as charity'.

Keyes had with him 36 men in total, around three-quarters of his original fighting force, but they were also short of much vital equipment – including rations and ammunition. Throughout the morning Keyes, in consultation

16 NOVEMBER 1941
0400hrs

Talisman aborts landing because of heavy seas

with Laycock, modified the plan of attack in light of the previous night's events. There were now to be just two raiding parties, rather than the four originally anticipated. No. 1 Detachment, under the command of Keyes and comprising Capt Campbell and 17 ORs, was to attack the villa used by Rommel and the German HQ at Beda Littoria. No. 2 Detachment, led by Lt Roy Cooke and consisting of six ORs, was to attack the Italian HQ at Cirene. This had been the intended target for David Sutherland, the demolitions expert, but neither he nor most of his explosives had made it ashore. As already arranged, Haselden was to cut communications on the road from Lamluda to El Faidia, while Laycock was to remain at the rendezvous with a sergeant and two ORs. Their job was to guard the stores and collect any more Commandos who might come ashore from *Talisman* (in fact, none did, as the weather failed to improve in the next 24 hours, compelling Miers to instruct Willmott not to try to land any more Commandos). It was also decided that on their return from the raid, the Commandos would rally at the rendezvous 1 mile inland, and not on the beach. Once Keyes was satisfied with the amended plan he summoned his men and, according to Campbell:

> … after explaining the new plan in outline, supervised the opening, repacking and distribution of the ammunition, explosives and rations. Although his original plan had been very thoroughly upset and his force lacked guides, two, or it may have been three, officers and some twenty men, Keyes gave no sign of being disturbed by this, and none of the men seemed to realise how seriously hampered the operation was from the outset.

THE RAID

Towards Beda Littoria

A new plan was in place by the afternoon of 16 November, but Keyes still had the problem of what to do about acquiring guides to lead them 18 miles south to the target at Beda Littoria. The two guides recruited from the Libyan Arab Force had been on *Talisman* and were presumed to have drowned. Haselden loaned his Arab guide to Keyes, saying he would pick up a replacement from Hussein Taher in Slonta. Haselden then set off across the *Jebel el-Akhdar*, and shortly after 1900hrs Keyes and his men followed.

The morning of 16 November had been bright and sunny, but it proved to be the calm before another storm descended on the Libyan Desert. By the afternoon the sky was dark and moody, and rain began to fall shortly before dusk, puzzling the raiders, who had been assured in their operational

Once ashore, Keyes and his depleted raiding party had to negotiate what is known locally as the *Jebel el-Akhdar* ('green mountain' in Arabic). In reality, it was a two-tier escarpment with a sloping shelf of land between the tiers in which lie innumerable gullies and dry riverbeds, as seen in this 2012 photograph. (Photograph courtesy Steve Hamilton – Western Desert Battlefield Tours)

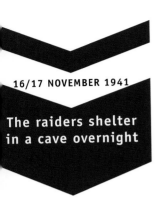

briefings that the weather would be temperate. None of the Commandos wore winter clothing. Instead, most wore civilian clothes under a battledress blouse and trousers with short puttees, and Army-issue boots. The officers carried either .45 Colt automatics or .38 Smith & Wesson revolvers, and the men .45 Thompson submachine guns, and clasp knives and whistles were on the end of lanyards tucked in the breast pocket of their battledress. In the haversacks slung over their shoulders, the men had rations (sardines, salmon, chocolate and fruit salad) as well as spare socks, water bottle, mess tin, hand grenades and sand-coloured lightweight blankets. In addition, most had a pair of crepe-soled plimsolls that were known as 'sand-creepers'.

'None of us had seen cloudy skies or rain for many months,' recounted Campbell. 'We had hoped for the usual dry North African weather, since we would have to spend about six days in the open. Whatever he may have felt like inside himself, Keyes certainly appeared confident and cheerful as we set off'. Col Laycock waved off the raiders, remaining behind in the *wadi* with Lt Pryor and Cpl John Brittlebank of the SBS, and another soldier armed with a Bren gun. Led by the guide, and with Drori the interpreter at his side, Keyes and his men climbed up the first tier of the escarpment and were on the 'step' by 2130hrs. 'All that night we marched inland over extremely difficult going, mostly rock-strewn sheep tracks,' said Campbell.

Our guide left us about midnight, fearing to go any further in our company. Keyes then had the difficult task of finding the way by the aid of an indifferent Italian map, his compass and an occasional sight of the stars. In spite of this responsibility he kept the heavily laden party going with my help and that of Lieutenant Roy Cooke.

Their progress slowed by the flight of their guide, the raiding party continued their trek south throughout the early hours of 17 November. Shortly before sunrise, Keyes called a halt to the march on top of a small hill marked on his Italian map as 'Um Girba'. Sentries were posted and the rest of the men covered themselves in their blankets and went to sleep.

Encountering the Senussi
Campbell was woken a couple of hours later by the sound of voices. Crawling out from under his blanket into a soft drizzle, he joined Keyes, who was sitting wrapped in his blanket listening to a breathless Drori explain that they were surrounded by armed Arabs. 'Raising our heads cautiously above the scrub we saw a few rascally-looking Arabs, one or two brandishing short Italian rifles,' said Campbell. He continued:

However, Keyes decided that they did not appear either particularly formidable or implacably hostile, so he gave the order for the chief of the band to be brought to him for a talk. Shortly afterwards a villainous-looking Arab, with a red head-cloth wound round his head, was brought up by the Palestinian interpreter and a sentry. Keyes exchanged a few civilities with this seedy brigand, and then began a conversation through the interpreter, asking his help against the hated Italians.

The leader of the band of Arabs was a man called Musa of the Dorsa tribe, who had been alerted to the presence of the Commandos by a local out looking for some stray cows on the morning of 17 November. Keyes took a letter from the pocket of his battledress from Seyed Idris, exiled chief of all the Senussi, and handed it to Musa. He couldn't read, however, so Drori read out its contents:

In the name of God, the Merciful. To my brethren, Sons of Heroes, People of Libya. The bearers of this letter are working with us, and in the holy cause of our country. Therefore, I bid you all, the people of Libya, who have the opportunity of meeting the bearers of this letter to afford them protection and help with all your strength. We beseech the Almighty that this, your work, may be crowned with victory. We greet you with the blessing of God.

KING IDRIS

Born at Al Jaghbub, the heartland of the Senussi territory, on 12 March 1889, Idris became Chief of the Senussi in 1916 following the abdication of his cousin Sayyid Ahmed Sharif es Senussi. Chief Idris was a staunch advocate of independence for Cyrenaica and was recognized as Emir of Tripolitania by the Italians in 1922. However, he soon declared war on Mussolini and Italy, fleeing into exile in Egypt from where he launched a campaign of guerrilla warfare against the colonialists.

Upon the outbreak of World War II, Idris offered his support to the British in their war against the Axis Powers in return for a promise of independence once the Italians had been defeated. Senussi tribesmen provided the British with vital intelligence on enemy troop movements and also carried out numerous acts of sabotage and ambushes on German and Italian convoys.

With the Allies victorious in North Africa in 1943, Idris returned to Benghazi, Cyrenaica, and his position as Emir. Following the end of the war Idris was awarded the Order of the Grand Cross of the British Empire in 1946 in recognition of his assistance in defeating the Axis Powers in Libya. In 1951 Idris was crowned King of Libya and 12 years later a revised constitution led to the renaming of his land, the Kingdom of Libya. Always a loyal friend to the British and Americans, King Idris led his country into an era of great prosperity until ill health forced his abdication in September 1969, but before Crown Prince Hasan

as-Senussi could accede to the throne, a group of Libyan Army officers under the leadership of Muammar Gaddafi staged a coup and abolished the monarchy. King Idris fled – once more – into exile in Egypt and died there in 1983, aged 94. Gaddafi's despotic rule ended with his death in 2011.

A Senussi warrior. Having resisted French and Italian colonialism in the years before World War I, the Senussi fought against the British in 1914–18. In World War II, however, the Senussi allied themselves with the British in the face of Italian and German aggression. (IWM E 10186)

The 18-mile approach to the target was over rough and rocky terrain, made worse by one of the worst storms in years that brought with it a torrent of rain. 'The going became so bad that we were compelled to go in single file to avoid knocking one another over as we slipped and stumbled through the mud,' recalled Capt Robin Campbell. (Photograph courtesy Steve Hamilton – Western Desert Battlefield Tours)

On hearing what Idris had to say, Musa broke into a broad grin and offered the Commandos whatever help he could. The first thing Keyes asked for was cigarettes, handing over some Italian lire in exchange for some cartons as he explained theirs had been ruined during their landing. Then Keyes got down to business with the leader, explained Campbell:

> After prolonged haggling, he [Musa] and Awad Mohammed Gibril of the Masamir tribe, a taller, younger, but equally unprepossessing ruffian, agreed to take the raiders to Rommel's Head Quarters, which they knew well, for the sum of a thousand Italian lire. They promised that when night fell they would guide the party to a cave within a few hours march of their objective, and in the meantime, for another thousand lire, offered to prepare a kid for them to eat. This offer was accepted thankfully, as the men had nothing hot to eat or drink since they had landed. When it grew dark we fell in and marched off in file, with Keyes and the guides and interpreter at the head.

The raiders marched south, but their progress was interrupted by some shouts away to their flank. Keyes dispatched a scout to see what the hullabaloo was about while they lay on the ground in the darkness. The scout returned and told Keyes he had seen nothing untoward and whoever had been shouting had dispersed. The men pressed on and after nearly three hours, reached a cave called Karem Gadeh at Carmel Hassan. They were now approximately 5 miles north of Beda Littoria. 'The entrance to the cave went down under a pile of stones and rocks,' recalled Campbell.

Inside it was fairly roomy and quite dry. Apart from an appalling smell of goats, it was an ideal place to spend the rest of the night and the following day. The roof was blackened by the smoke from generations of goatherds' fires, and the smell of generations of goats clung to the floor and walls. Keyes decided it would be safe to light a fire inside, so that we passed the rest of the night in a dry and warm though smoky cave.

The guides left the Commandos in the cave with a promise to return before dawn, which they did, warning Keyes that they should soon be on the move because it was a custom of goatherds to bring their flocks to the cave when the weather was bad. Keyes heeded the advice, moving his men to a nearby copse where there was an abundance of cyclamen growing and some arbutus berries, a fruit similar to the strawberry and called the 'Fruit of God' by the Senussi. Leaving Campbell in charge of the party, Keyes, together with Sgt Jack Terry and Lt Roy Cooke, went off with one of the guides, called Awad, to spy out the land.

Reconnoitring the target

Terry was another veteran of No. 11 (Scottish) Commando, though there was little Scottish about the 20-year-old. *Born in* Bulwell, Nottinghamshire, he became an apprentice butcher upon leaving school after being turned down by the police force on account of his size. In 1937 he enlisted in the Royal Artillery and was a member of the British Expeditionary Force, being sent to France in the spring of 1940. After being plucked from the beaches at Dunkirk, Terry volunteered for the Commandos and saw action at Litani River.

The account given after the war by the Senussi to Keyes' sister described how:

In the morning the leader [Keyes] asked Awad to get some Arab clothes so that both he and Awad might go to Beda Littoria in disguise. Awad refused because of the number of enemy spies and agents about and took them to the wood to hide. The leader wanted to examine Beda Littoria through his binoculars but could not do so because they were on low ground.

What Keyes was able to see, however, was the top of the second escarpment, beyond which was the objective, approximately a mile further on. Determined to gather as much intelligence as possible, Keyes persuaded Awad to send his son into Beda Littoria, promising him a reward of some lire if he brought back good information. Not long after the boy had embarked on his espionage mission, a thunderstorm swept in from the coast, bringing with it a deluge of rain. Keyes decided to risk moving the party from the copse back to the cave in order that they should spend the hours preparatory to the attack as dry as possible. The men made themselves as comfortable as they could in the cave and then settled down to wait. Some fed on their rations, tinned salmon and fruit salad, while others cleaned and checked their weapons.

In the afternoon the boy returned from Beda Littoria, bringing with him much valuable information. 'His report enabled Keyes to draw an

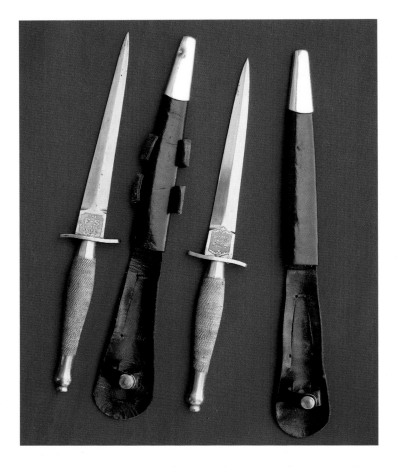

The Commandos were issued with the 1st Pattern Fairbairn-Sykes Dagger; this formidable weapon had a 6⁷/₈in double-edged blade, and has remained an iconic special-forces weapon to this day. (Leroy Thompson)

excellent sketch map, which proved to be extremely accurate and included such details as the outbuildings, and the park for staff cars,' said Campbell. 'He was thus able to give the men a good visual notion of their objective. The boy told him there was a guard-tent in the grounds of the headquarters, but that if it rained the guards would probably all be inside the house'.

Armed with the precious information, Keyes drew up his final plan of attack, detailing individual tasks to each member of the raiding party. He, Campbell and Terry would enter Rommel's villa in search of their prey, while three ORs were to disable the electric light plant. Five men were to act as lookouts at the exits from the guard tent and the car park. The rest of the party were dispersed so as to prevent interference by the enemy: two were posted outside the hotel a few hundred yards from the villa to prevent anyone leaving, and another two soldiers were detailed to watch the road on each side of the house. The other two Commandos would guard the entrance used by Keyes to gain access to the villa. Keyes told all of his men that the password challenge would be 'Island' to be answered by 'Arran'.

The loss of the majority of soldiers from *Talisman* did present a problem to Keyes, however, as he could not address the threat posed by the presence of another barracks half a mile to the south. He did not have enough men to nullify this threat and instead counted on their achieving their aims with such speed that the men from this barracks wouldn't have time to come to Rommel's rescue. With this in mind, Keyes modified Cooke's role in the operation. Instead of leaving the main party on top of the escarpment and heading towards the Italian HQ at Cirene, Cooke and his five men would now accompany Keyes to Beda Littoria and guard the road east of the villa until the moment they heard the first gunfire. Only then were they to strike out east towards their objective.

With each Commando fully briefed on his own role in the impending mission, the men then submitted themselves to a foot inspection. One soldier, Bob Fowler of The Queen's Own Cameron Highlanders, had trodden on a rusty nail shortly after landing on the beach and his leg was now so swollen that Keyes ordered him to remain in the cave and guard their surplus kit. Before the men enjoyed a final meal of bread and marmalade, they covered their faces in black cork and changed from their boots into their plimsolls. Some of the men slipped canvas ammunition bandoliers under their battledress to keep the sticks of gelignite they contained dry.

Approaching the target

Then, at 1800hrs, they left the cave, Keyes deciding to allow six hours to cover the 5 miles to the target because of the dreadful weather conditions. Throughout the afternoon the rain had fallen in torrents and now the terrain was ankle-deep in mud. 'Spirits were sinking – I know mine were – at the prospect of a long, cold, wet and muddy march before we even arrived at the starting point of a hazardous operation,' recalled Campbell.

> … it became so dark it was only just possible to see the man in front. We had to hold on to one another's bayonet scabbards in order to keep in touch. Every now and again a man would fall, and the whole column would have to halt while he picked himself up. From time to time the middle of the column would lose touch with the man in front of him, and we would have to stop and sort ourselves out again. We reached the bottom of the escarpment at about 10.30 p.m. without serious mishap. After a short rest we began our climb of about 500 feet of muddy turf with outcropping rocks. About half way up the noise of a man slipping and striking his tommy gun against a rock roused a watch-dog, and a stream of light issued from the door of a hut as it was flung open about a hundred yards away on our flank. As we crouched motionless, hardly breathing, we heard a man shouting at the dog. Finally the door closed, and we resumed our way upward. At the summit (which is known as Zaidan hill) we found a cart track which the guides said led straight to the back of the German Headquarters. We halted for a rest and Keyes re-formed the men, some twenty-four all told.

A rugged US-manufactured sidearm offering lethal stopping power, the .45-calibre Colt M1911 semi-automatic pistol was a standard-issue weapon employed by the Commandos during World War II. (Leroy Thompson)

Having rested for a few minutes, the raiders pushed off down the cart track with Keyes in the lead, followed by Terry, Drori and the Arabs. Some 50 yards back were Campbell and the rest of the Commandos. As they neared the bottom of the cart track the guides became≈increasingly nervous, telling Drori that they wished to depart, as their job was done. The interpreter told Keyes the men's concerns, whereupon he took out his revolver and said to Drori: 'Tell them to go on until I tell them to stop'. Continuing along the cart track, which was muddy but otherwise easily negotiable, the Commandos came to a shrub beside a fork. They were now less than half a mile from Beda Littoria but, despite their proximity to the target, Keyes allowed those who wanted it a final cigarette. Then they moved on, creeping ever closer until they reached the track that led down the slope and towards the rear of the village.

THE RAID ON BEDA LITTORIA

16–18 NOVEMBER 1941

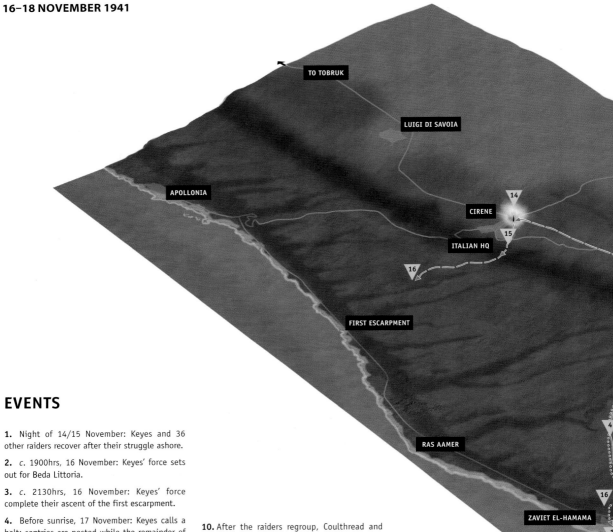

TO TOBRUK

LUIGI DI SAVOIA

APOLLONIA

CIRENE

14

15

ITALIAN HQ

16

FIRST ESCARPMENT

RAS AAMER

4

16

ZAVIET EL-HAMAMA

1

CHESCEM EL-K

EVENTS

1. Night of 14/15 November: Keyes and 36 other raiders recover after their struggle ashore.

2. *c.* 1900hrs, 16 November: Keyes' force sets out for Beda Littoria.

3. *c.* 2130hrs, 16 November: Keyes' force complete their ascent of the first escarpment.

4. Before sunrise, 17 November: Keyes calls a halt; sentries are posted while the remainder of Keyes' party rests.

5. 1800hrs, 17 November: Keyes' men leave the Karem Gadeh cave at Carmel Hassan, heading for Beda Littoria.

6. At the crest of the second escarpment, Keyes' party splits; Lt Cooke's party heads for the communications mast at Cirene, while the main party enters Beda Littoria.

7. Keyes details two raiders to block the path leading from the Carabinieri barracks to the villa.

8. The raiders find that the back door of the villa is blocked and cannot gain entry.

9. Shortly before midnight, 17 November: Keyes, Terry and Campbell force their way through the front door and a firefight breaks out in the hallway; Keyes is killed.

10. After the raiders regroup, Coulthread and Bruce destroy the electric light plant with explosives.

11. Bruce places explosive time pencils in vehicles located in the villa's car park.

12. During the raiders' withdrawal, Boxhammer is killed by a shot to the stomach.

13. Leaving the seriously wounded Campbell behind, Terry leads the surviving raiders back toward the beach.

14. During the attack on the villa, Cooke's party blows up the communications tower at Cirene.

15. Cooke's party takes refuge in Cirene's ancient tombs before heading towards the coast.

16. Resting in a cave en route to the beach, Cooke's party is surrounded by enemy troops and surrenders after exchanging fire.

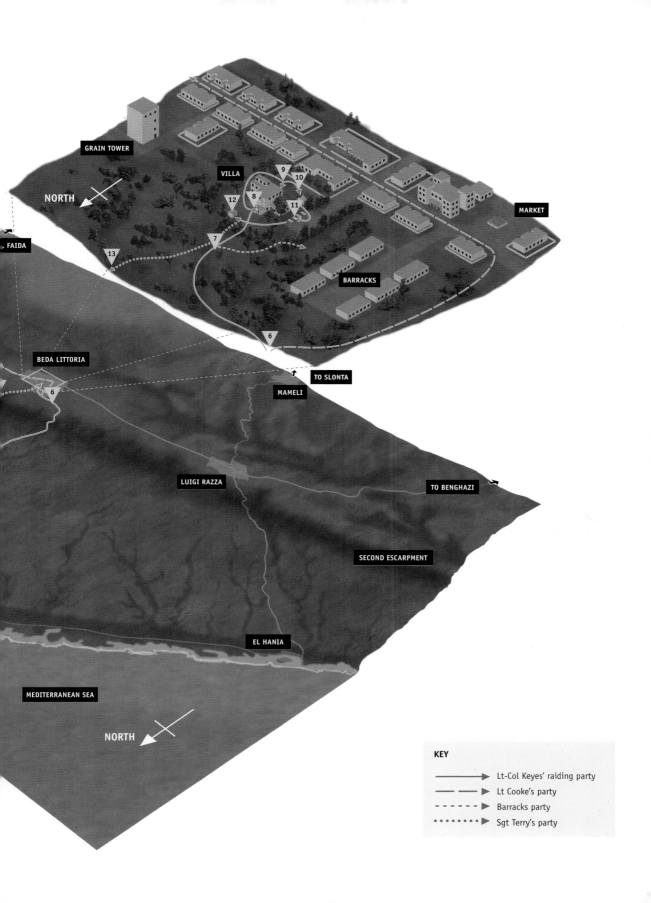

GRAIN TOWER

VILLA

NORTH

9

10

12

8

11

MARKET

FAIDA

7

13

BARRACKS

6

BEDA LITTORIA

TO SLONTA

MAMELI

6

LUIGI RAZZA

TO BENGHAZI

SECOND ESCARPMENT

EL HANIA

MEDITERRANEAN SEA

NORTH

KEY

Lt-Col Keyes' raiding party

Lt Cooke's party

Barracks party

Sgt Terry's party

Close by was a solitary cedar tree and here Keyes told Lt Cooke to take his five men and move into position on the main road. Keyes, meanwhile, from his vantage point, called over one of the guides. He could clearly see the imposing grain tower, which rose above the surrounding flat countryside, as well as the six-storey prefecture, but he asked the guide to point out Rommel's villa and the barracks housing a detachment of the Carabinieri, Italy's military police.

Approximately 100 yards from the barracks was the *suk*, the market, separated from it by a barbed-wire fence and a hedge. Cedar and eucalyptus trees lined the road leading through the village towards the prefecture, in front of which was the main square. There was an ornate fountain in the square and a rostrum on one side from which Italian officials frequently harangued the locals. With the exception of the traditional *suk*, Beda Littoria was a modern village, consisting of buildings constructed by the Italians in the last 20 years.

At this point the guides categorically refused to go any further and Keyes, realizing he had no further need for them, instructed them to return up the track and wait by the cedar tree. They would receive their money once the raid was over. As the guides melted into the darkness, Keyes took Terry on a preliminary reconnaissance of the target. 'While he was away one of my party tripped over a tin can and roused a dog, which began to bark,' recounted Campbell.

An Arab in one of the houses also began to scream. After a minute or two an Italian in uniform and an Arab officer of the Italian Libyan Arab Force emerged from one of the huts and approached us, asking who we were and what we were doing there. Drori replied in German saying, 'We are German troops on patrol. Go away and keep your dog quiet.' Drori repeated this in Arabic, asking them to quiet the man in the hut, and the Arab officer, believing they were Germans, then spoke to the man who was screaming, addressing him by name and told him to be quiet. Bidding us 'Gute Nacht' they disappeared back into their hut apparently satisfied, which the men thought was a great joke.

The Germans at Beda Littoria

The Commandos wouldn't have laughed if they knew that the villa in their sights didn't in fact contain the top German commander in North Africa. Nor did it even house its usual occupant, Major Schleusener, Rommel's quartermaster-general, who was in an Apollonia hospital suffering from dysentery, the same hospital in which his deputy, Hauptmann (Captain) Otto, was being treated for inflammation of the lungs. Instead, Hauptmann Weiss was the senior officer in charge on the night of 17/18 November, and under his command were a 'couple of dozen officers, orderlies, runners, drivers and the usual personnel to be found on a Quartermaster's staff'.

In fact, Rommel had never used the villa at Beda Littoria as his private accommodation. At the end of July 1941, when he had been given command of the newly formed Panzergruppe Afrika, Rommel had his GHQ in Beda Littoria with Generalmajor Alfred Gause, his chief of staff, and Oberstleutnant Siegfried Westphal, *Ia* (Operations). Their offices were in the prefecture and the houses close by the impressive white building contained their staff officers.

In August Schleusener took up residency at Beda Littoria and Rommel relocated his HQ to the Gambut landing ground between Tobruk and Bardia, about 200 miles east of the villa. According to Rommel's aide-de-camp, Heinz Schmidt, the Luftwaffe (German Air Force) garrison at Gambut had 'transformed an old underground *bir* [well] into their mess. The ancient cistern was comfortable and bomb-proof, and was completely equipped with ante-room and bar-counter that had been moved from buildings at El Adem' (Schmidt 1951: 96). The mess was lavishly equipped, with iced drinks, fresh fruit and cigarettes readily available for Rommel and his staff.

The villa at Beda Littoria had 'been intended to serve as a refuge for Rommel where he could get away from his own staff and the problems of war from time to time' (Schmidt 1951: 98). The German commander had indeed stayed a night or two at the villa in the past, and Schmidt recalled a convivial dinner at which Rommel, Gause and Marshal Ugo Cavallero, chief of the Italian Supreme Command, had been present.

Not only was Rommel not in the villa on the night of the attack – he wasn't even in North Africa. He was in Rome, with his wife, having celebrated his 50th birthday two days previously, and on the 17th he and Frau Rommel were at the opera as guests of Generalleutnant Johann von Ravenstein, Rommel's second-in-command in the desert, who was also enjoying a few days' rest and recuperation in the Italian capital. According to Schmidt, as they were leaving the opera, Ravenstein asked Rommel if he had enjoyed the performance, to which his superior replied: 'We must shift those battalions in the Medawwa sector' (quoted in Schmidt 1951: 98).

At the villa, however, a late-night conference was in progress on the evening of the 17th, chaired by Weiss and attended by an engineer officer and two supply officers named Schulz and Ampt. Security at the villa was lax, understandably, as the Germans were 250 miles behind their own lines. A military policeman called Jamatter 'kept watch in the corridor below [and] his sole weapon was a bayonet. He was less a guard than a distributor of late-arriving mail' (Carell 1961: 49). Another soldier, a 20-year-old from Bavaria called Matthew Boxhammer of the quartermaster's motorized section, was lying on a camp bed in the guard tent (a big bell-tent) and in a workroom on the ground floor of the villa were Leutnant Kaufholz, a liaison officer, plus Feldwebel Leutzen, Unteroffizier Kovacic and another NCO named Bartl. These four men were asleep on makeshift camp beds in the workroom, preferring to billet at the villa rather than in the barracks with their Italian allies.

The attack begins

When Keyes and Terry returned from their reconnaissance Keyes informed Bdr Joe Kearney, Sgt Charlie Bruce and Pte Denis Coulthread – who had been tasked with cutting telephone wires – that there was a change of plan: they were to cover the rear of the villa and kill whoever came or went out of the back door, which Keyes had found to be locked. Keyes ordered the

**17 NOVEMBER 1941
1800hrs**

**The raiders depart
for the villa**

**18 NOVEMBER 1941
0045hrs**

**The attack on the
villa begins**

Unable to force their way through a window, Keyes, Campbell and Terry had to go in through the front door of the villa, seen here in 2012. Campbell, a fluent German-speaker, knocked on the door and demanded entrance – not the best way to launch a guerrilla operation. (Photograph courtesy Steve Hamilton – Western Desert Battlefield Tours)

rest of the men to move into their positions, and then a few minutes before midnight he led his raiding party through a hedge and into the garden of the villa. The first task was to eliminate the guard inside the guard tent, Boxhammer. Accounts differ as to how Boxhammer met his end, with German reports describing how he was shot dead at the end of the raid, but Elizabeth Keyes, sister of Geoffrey, wrote that her brother 'went forward alone and killed the guard'. The fact that Boxhammer was shot in the stomach suggests he was killed while the raiders escaped, when stealth was no longer important.

'All the ground floor windows were high up and barred with heavy wooden shutters, so it was impossible to get in that way,' recalled Campbell.

> There was no alternative but to use the front door. We followed [Keyes] round the building on to a gravel sweep in front of the house. The front door was set back inside a porch, at the top of a flight of stone steps. Keyes ran up the steps. He was carrying a Colt, and I knocked on the door for him, demanding loudly in German to be let in. The door opened on a second pair of glass doors, and we were confronted by a German.

The German was Jamatter, the military policeman, armed only with a bayonet but a brave bear of a man. 'Keyes at once closed with him, covering him with his Colt,' said Campbell.

> The man seized the muzzle of Keyes' revolver and tried to wrest it from him. Before I or Terry could get round behind him he retreated, still holding on to Keyes, to a position with his back to the wall, and his either side protected by the first and second pairs of

> doors at the entrance. He started to shout. Keyes could not draw a knife and neither I nor Terry could get round Keyes, as the doors were in the way.

Jamatter was too strong for Keyes and he slammed the British officer against a door, waking up Leutzen, Kaufholz, Bartl and Kovacic. The four men jumped from their beds and grabbed their weapons. Realizing the operation had already gone awry, Campbell closed on the courageous Jamatter and shot the German with his .38 revolver. The element of surprise was gone and the three raiders knew time was now of the essence. 'We found ourselves, when we had time to look round, in a large hall with a stone floor, it had a stone stairway leading to the upper stories on the right,' said Campbell.

> We heard a man in heavy boots clattering down the stairs though we could not see him nor he us, as he was hidden by a right hand turn in the stairway. He was shouting 'What goes on there?' As he came to the turn and his feet came in sight, Sergeant Terry fired a burst with his tommy-gun. The man turned and fled away upstairs.

According to the subsequent German report just as Terry fired his burst at the man on the stairway, Leutzen emerged from the workroom on the ground floor and was confronted by Campbell and his .38 Smith & Wesson. 'Leutzen jumped to one side and tried to take cover,' ran the report. 'Lieut. Kaufholz, who by now had stepped up next to Leutzen, returned the fire, but fell to the ground having been hit himself several times. Two of the intruders chose this moment to enter the room and throw two hand grenades'.

In his version of events, Campbell recalled that Keyes flung open a couple of doors on either side of the hall, but the room beyond each of these was empty. Then, seeing a crack of light under one door, he opened it and

Jamatter was probably armed with the German armed forces' standard-issue rifle bayonet, the Seitengewehr (Sidearm) 94/98. This weapon had a 9.9in blade that was 1in wide at the hilt. (© Royal Armouries PR.10224)

'fired two or three rounds with his Colt .45 automatic'. It was Campbell's suggestion to throw in a grenade (one, and not the two mentioned in the German account) so while Keyes held the door shut, the captain removed the pin from a grenade. 'I said "Right" and Keyes opened the door,' said Campbell. 'I threw in the grenade, which I saw roll to the middle of the room, and Sergeant Terry gave a burst with his Tommy-gun'.

As Campbell threw the grenade into the room Keyes yelled 'well done'. The next instant there was a burst of machine-gun fire. 'A bullet struck him just over the heart and he fell unconscious at the feet of myself and Terry,' said Campbell.

> After the grenade went off, this was followed by complete silence, and we could see that the light in the room had gone out. I decided Keyes had to be moved, in case there was further fighting in the building (and because we intended to blow it up), so between us Sergeant Terry and I carried him outside and laid him on the grass verge to the left of the front door. He must have died as we were carrying him outside, for when I felt his heart it had ceased to beat.

Paul Karl Schmidt, an SS officer who worked as Joachim von Ribbentrop's press spokesman as well as for Joseph Goebbels' press department, spoke to some of the Germans present on the night of the raid and wrote that the grenade knocked Leutzen over, but the German was unhurt. Kovacic, who was on his way to the door, received the full impact of the blast and lay dead on the tiles. A third NCO, Bartl, who was about to jump out of bed, was able to fall back and remained unscathed. Presumably it was Bartl's return fire that mortally wounded Keyes.

The commotion on the ground floor had brought Weiss, Schulz and Ampt running from their conference on the first floor. Having instructed his orderly to hide all-important documents, Weiss and his fellow officers armed themselves with pistols and crept along the landing in darkness

Taken in 2012, this photograph shows the hallway of the villa where Keyes was shot. The main entrance to the villa is to the left, and Keyes would have grappled with Jamatter before, in all probability, being shot accidentally by Capt Robin Campbell. (Photograph courtesy Steve Hamilton –Western Desert Battlefield Tours)

At the back of the villa, seen here, Denis Coulthread and Charles Bruce were unable to force their way inside. Instead, they stood guard and, along with Drori, the interpreter, shot dead Jäger in his pyjamas. (Photo courtesy Steve Hamilton – Western Desert Battlefield Tours)

towards the top of the stairs. When Ampt first shone his torch down the staircase, its beam picked out Keyes, lying motionless on the floor. He switched off the torch and told Weiss what he had seen. A minute later, when Ampt illuminated the ground floor once more, the body had been removed. 'Everything was quiet,' ran the German report.

The door of the house had been closed again. Groans were to be heard coming from the workroom... On entering the room the two officers [Ampt and Schulz] found that the floor was covered with water, which was flowing from the central heating apparatus, damaged by the explosion of the hand grenades [sic]. The water was mixed with blood. Lieut. Kaufholz was lying on the ground with severe gunshot wounds, and Rifleman Kovacic was lying on his bed. They both appeared to be severely wounded.

THE DEATH OF KEYES (OVERLEAF)

After Robin Campbell banged on the door of the villa and demanded entry, a military policeman called Jamatter, armed only with a bayonet, opened the door. He was pounced on by Keyes, smaller but carrying a Colt pistol. The pair grappled in the hallway and Jamatter cleverly used Keyes to shield himself from Campbell. Meanwhile, Terry fired a burst from his submachine gun up the flight of steps leading to the first floor. The commotion alerted three other Germans billeted on the ground floor and, sensing that they were in danger of losing the initiative, Campbell opened fire with his .38 revolver. According to the contemporary British version of events, with Jamatter disabled the raiders proceeded to hurl grenades into the rooms on the ground floor. It was then that Keyes was mortally wounded by a burst of fire from inside one of the rooms. However, in recent years there has been speculation that Campbell accidentally shot and killed Keyes during the struggle with Jamatter, a theory that Terry didn't deny shortly before his death in 2006.

Meanwhile, at the back of the villa, Denis Coulthread and Charles Bruce were standing guard by the back door, behind which was a small office that had formerly served as a kitchen. It was crammed full of files and office tables; at the back of the room was a spiral staircase into the cellar, which served as the sleeping quarters for Alfons Hirsch and another NCO. In fact, the back door had no lock, so the pair improvised each night by pushing a barrel of water up against the door.

Coulthread spotted the yellow disc of a torch dancing through the darkness. The torch was held by an Oberleutnant Jäger, whose own workroom was separated by a partition of three-ply wood from the one destroyed by the Commandos. On hearing the gunfire Jäger had jumped out of the window in his pyjamas, taking his torch and his sidearm with him.

Coulthread wasn't alone in spotting the danger. Drori, the interpreter, also saw the beam of the torch through the driving rain and pressed himself against the wall of the villa, his rifle at the ready. When Jäger was 10 yards away, Drori stepped out of the shadows and fired. 'I just stood there and he very obligingly walked onto the end of my gun. All I had to do was pull the trigger,' Drori told Coulthread. 'The German did not shout or sigh, but fell down silently'.

A few moments later Campbell and Terry emerged from the building, carrying Keyes. Drori asked if he could be of any assistance. 'No,' replied Campbell. 'He's dead.'

Drori then gestured to the German he had just shot dead and Campbell congratulated the interpreter on his kill. 'Are we going to retreat, sir?' Drori asked Campbell.

'No,' said the captain.

According to Drori's account he was ordered to remain with the body of Keyes by Campbell, who returned to the front entrance of the villa with Jack Terry. Suddenly, there was a burst of gunfire, followed by a groan and an urgent shout from Terry. Drori dashed round the side of the villa and discovered that Campbell had been shot in the shinbone by one of his own men, who had mistaken him for a German.

The raiders take stock

An example of the explosive time pencil – officially the 'Switch, time delay, No 10 "Pencil"'. (© Imperal War Museum MUN 1967)

While Terry administered morphine to treat Campbell's badly shattered leg, the captain ordered Kearney and Coulthread to blow up what they could with their sticks of gelignite. These explosives were taped together and at one end was a fuse with a large brimstone head. Kearney lit the fuse

and threw the gelignite through the window left open by Jäger. Another Commando, Spike Hughes, lobbed an incendiary bomb into the room, but neither device detonated.

Meanwhile, Coulthread and Charlie Bruce had turned their attention to the electric light plant; they could hear the hum of a generator behind a large steel door. Unfortunately, the rain had dampened their fuses and the matches they carried inside their battledress, so Terry suggested they stuff the explosives into an external pipe, followed by a hand grenade. This plan worked, the light plant exploding with a muffled roar.

Terry told Bruce to take some of their explosive time pencils and plant them among the vehicles in the car park. This device was a slim, 6in-long glass tube with a spring-loaded striker held in place by a strip of copper wire. At the top was a glass phial containing acid, which broke when gently squeezed. The acid then ate through the wire and released the striker. The thicker the wire, the longer the delay before the striker was triggered, and the pencils were colour-coded according to the length of fuse.

While Bruce set off towards the car park, Terry blew his whistle, the signal for the Commandos to begin their withdrawal. The morphine had

A member of the LRDG driving a jeep in 1942. Cooke's party initially headed east towards the Italian headquarters at Cirene in the expectation of rendezvousing with an LRDG patrol. 'Unfortunately, with the weather and the late hour, we were unable to get the lift we expected on the road,' said Cooke. (IWM CBM 1212)

18 NOVEMBER 1941
0315hrs

Lt Cooke and party attack target at the Cirene crossroads

dulled the pain from Campbell's broken leg but the captain knew he was in no fit state to march the 18 miles back to the rendezvous; nor could he expect his men to carry him with the enemy on their trail. Campbell therefore handed command of the raiding party to Terry. After saying a hurried farewell to Campbell, the raiders 'left him propped against a tree at the back of the house, and he gave them a map and all his remaining ammunition and explosives'.

Terry had been unable to find Bruce since he had set off towards the car park, and Charles Lock, Bob Murray and Jimmy Bogle also failed to appear at the sound of the whistle. Unable to wait any longer, Terry led the remaining 11 raiders north, stumbling through the dark for more than a mile until Terry disappeared over the edge of a gulley. Fortunately for the sergeant, a bush saved him from a nasty fall, but he lost his Thompson in the incident; it was decided that the party would lie up for the rest of the night rather than risking any further mishap.

Lt Cooke's party

After leaving Keyes, Cooke and his five men, among them two soldiers called Gornall and Paxton, watched the main road until they heard the first sounds of gunfire from the villa. The raiders began marching as quickly as possible along the road. A large house with a garage offered the possibility of acquiring transport, but it was found to be impossible to break into the garage without giving away their presence so they continued on foot. Knowing that they had to blow up the pylon (approximately 8 miles from Beda Littoria) before sunrise, Cooke decided to stop the first vehicle that came along the road.

For nearly an hour no vehicle appeared, but then eventually they heard an engine in the distance. Gornall stood in the road and flagged the vehicle to stop, but the two Italian soldiers inside had heard over the radio of the attack at Beda Littoria. Momentarily slowing down as it approached Gornall, the lorry then accelerated and the Commando was forced to jump for his life. Cooke and the rest of the men opened fire, resulting in the vehicle swerving off the road 15 yards away. Despite desperate attempts to start the lorry, the Commandos found it impossible and so, after binding the two terrified Italians, the raiders continued down the road. The blistering pace set by Cooke took its toll on the men. 'We had to drop off two of the boys as they couldn't make it. One of them had lost his shoes and his feet were in a fearful state,' he said. 'However, we filled them up with grenades, etc. and told them to muck up any odd transport, or what have you, that they could find, and try to get back'.

At 0300hrs Cooke and his remaining three men reached the communications pylon, but were then confronted by the same problem experienced a couple of hours earlier by their comrades outside the villa. 'All matches, etc. for setting off the charges were soaked, even inside the oilskin pouches,' said Cooke. 'I tried a grenade under the charge and then running like hell and falling flat and felt very foolish when it turned out a blind. The second one went off, but the charge didn't. I returned to the boys nearly frantic with wind up and frustration and nerves, cursing pretty profusely'.

It was Gornall who provided Cooke with the solution to his problem: 'I suppose a self-igniting incendiary wouldn't be any good sir, would it?' he said. Cooke congratulated the soldier on his initiative and a minute later the pylon went up in flames. After admiring their handiwork for no more than a second or two, Cooke and his men vanished into the darkness.

Manhunt

Within minutes of the Commandos' flight from the villa, dozens of Italian soldiers appeared from the barracks behind the town hall. 'Orders were given for a systematic search of the garden,' ran the German report on the raid. As well as discovering the bodies of Boxhammer, the young guard, and Jäger, the Germans also came across the wounded Campbell propped against a tree, 'and stood over him debating whether to finish him off'. Common sense prevailed, however, and the wounded man was brought inside for questioning. 'An attempted interrogation of the English officer, whilst still suffering from the shock of his wound, was unsuccessful, as it was impossible to get him to make a statement,' the report stated. Instead a different approach was tried, as described by Paul Karl Schmidt:

> Captain Campbell had received a shot from a tommy-gun or a revolver at close quarters which had completely smashed his shinbone in the centre... By rights the leg should have been amputated, since the prospect of healing was very small and the danger of infection very great. At his request, Doctor Werner Junge did not amputate and tried to save the leg. Since Junge spoke fluent English he was given orders to question Campbell. The latter did not betray the fact that he knew German. Junge could discover nothing of any importance. On the contrary, Campbell saw at once through the Doctor's game and said at last in German: 'You needn't bother – you won't get anything out of me.' (Carell 1961: 56)

With Campbell refusing to talk, the Germans had to make their own assumptions about the raiders, few of which were correct. 'Judging by their clothing, one comes to the conclusion that the Englishmen had been dropped from the air and belonged to an Airborne Unit,' Weitz said in his report. 'Both [Campbell and Keyes] had not shaved for several days and one could conclude that they had been dropped some time ago, and had chosen this day of particularly heavy rain as favourable for their undertaking'.

Just as the Germans had finished conducting their search of the garden and surrounding areas, word reached them of the sabotaged communications pylon and damaged truck on the road to Cirene. Weitz dispatched a patrol to ascertain what had happened and they discovered 'footprints on the ground [that] gave the impression that they were made by English rubber soled shoes'. At first light the manhunt began, the local Italian Carabinieri enlisting the help of locals by promising 'eighty pounds of corn and twenty pounds of sugar for each Britisher that you betray to us'. Among the excited throng of Arabs in Beda Littoria was Awad

The view from the conning tower of a T-class submarine, similar to that of HMS *Torbay* and *Talisman*. The stormy seas at Chescem el-Kelb meant that the Commandos had extreme difficulty launching their dinghies. (Cody Images)

Mohammed Gibril, one of the two guides who had been told to wait by the cedar tree. When none of the Commandos appeared he had crept into the village to discover what had unfolded. Now, in the early-morning rain, the market was full of 'German and Italian soldiers with armed police spread out like locusts going northwards'. Awad asked one of the market traders what all the fuss was about, and 'was told that the British had attacked Rommel's House but unfortunately Rommel was not there. The Arabs were laughing and were delighted with the exploit'.

Cooke and his men, having opened fire on the lorry, headed north-west, towards the ancient Greek tombs at the foot of the second escarpment. 'We lay up in an old tomb that day [18 November], very cold and wet we were,' he recalled:

> Pushed off next night to try and get back to the ship. We went very hard and got back to within five miles of the place, but at about 8.30 that morning had to rest, which we did in a cave with some Arabs. We didn't know it, but we had sat down in front of two battalions that were beating the scrub for us and looking in all the caves. The Arabs managed to slip out before we got the troops right on top of us, and tried to divert attention from the cave, by a little shooting on their own account, but no go. Two blokes came down into the cave and we shot them, then they threw down so much stuff at us that the fumes nearly suffocated us, so we called it a day.

Awad the guide, meanwhile, having seen the confusion in the market and the start of the German manhunt, quickly made his way back up the cart-track to the cave where Bob Fowler had been left to guard the stores. Fowler had already guessed something had gone badly wrong because he'd seen no sight of his comrades since they had left 12 hours earlier. Keyes' camera, which had several incriminating photos of the raiders, was buried deep in the mud along with a pair of field-glasses. Not long after Fowler had accomplished this task he was collected by Awad and together they set off to the beach.

A short distance behind Fowler and Awad was Charlie Bruce who, having laid his time pencils among the vehicles in the car park, had made his way away from Beda Littoria accompanied by Charles Lock, Bob Murray and Jimmy Bogle. The four Commandos reached the cave not long after Fowler had set out and on finding it empty, continued north. Headed in the same direction was the 12-strong party led by Terry, all of whom were by now tired, cold, wet and hungry. They were also aware that scores of enemy soldiers would now be swarming after them. It was a sobering thought as they made their weary way across the *Jebel el-Akhdar*.

Laycock and *Torbay*

Following the landings on 15 November, Lt-Cdr Miers, skipper of the submarine *Torbay*, had ordered *Talisman* back to Alexandria. So few raiders had got ashore that he would be able to transport them all back in his vessel, he told *Talisman*'s skipper, Michael Willmott. For the next two days *Torbay* remained off the beach at Chescem el-Kelb, lying on the bottom of the sea during the day and surfacing at night. On 17 November Miers had received a weather report 'which unfortunately did not even approximate to the prevailing weather conditions, which were most unfavourable' (PRO 2001: 289).

On the morning of the 18th, as the Commandos raced south from the villa, Miers surfaced and once again looked out from the conning tower on a storm-ravaged landscape, the sea lumpen with a swell running from the north. Suddenly an enemy aircraft was spotted in the distance (probably searching for the Commandos) and *Torbay* was forced to dive to the bottom, where it remained until 1900hrs.

At 1700hrs, two hours before *Torbay* surfaced, Terry and his 11 men had reached the rendezvous point in the *wadi* containing Laycock and his small party, who passed the time reading and doing crossword puzzles. Terry gave a potted account of the raid, describing the death of Keyes and the wound to Campbell, and also mentioned an encounter with a group of Italian native levies a few miles back. It was Drori's opinion that these men weren't to be trusted and had probably reported the Commandos' presence to Italian soldiers.

While Terry and the Commandos tucked into a meal of biscuits and bully beef, Laycock made his way to the beach to see if he could spot *Torbay*. First, however, he went to the cave where they had left the rubber dinghies and Mae Wests three days earlier. They were gone. As Laycock made his way

**18 NOVEMBER 1941
1700hrs**

Sgt Terry reaches rendezvous at wadi

18 NOVEMBER 1941
1900hrs

Laycock signals
***Torbay* from the**
beach

along the beach he saw an Arab watching from a distance. The man wasn't Senussi and when Laycock approached him, he took off. Unsettled by the loss of the dinghies and the stranger on the beach, Laycock sent word to the men in the *wadi* to move to the beach, leaving three men behind to wait for Cooke's party to arrive.

By now Bruce and his party of Commandos had also reached the *wadi* and the Commandos took up positions in some of the caves close to the beach. Counting the three men left in the *wadi*, Laycock had 21 men under his command, including two Arab guides. At 1900hrs Laycock spotted *Torbay* a quarter of a mile out to sea through his field glasses. Using his signal torch the colonel asked for some Mae Wests and a grass (towing) line to be delivered to the beach. From the conning tower of the submarine, Miers was troubled by the signal, although as agreed with Laycock he didn't respond to the signal with one of his own because of security precautions. He was at a loss to understand why the beach party should require life jackets when each Commando had landed wearing two Mae Wests.

Nevertheless, Miers obeyed the signal, instructing Lt Ingles and Cpl Severn of the SBS to prepare to paddle ashore in a folboat containing life jackets, food and a grass line. In addition:

> they also were to inform those on shore that the weather was unsuitable for boat work but was improving, and that in order not to delay re-embarkation, if a large proportion of the force was present, the *Torbay* would close at dawn to within 100 yards of the spit of sand at the western end of the beach, so that they could swim out to her. (PRO 2001: 290)

As Ingles and Severn prepared for their mission a second signal was received from the shore, informing Miers that the enemy was nowhere near the beach. The swell was by now so heavy that it proved impossible to launch the folboat, so at 2250hrs the two SBS men attempted to leave the casing of the submarine in a rubber dinghy. This, too, was not possible because of the heavy seas, but Miers decided to lash the 23 life jackets, 12 water bottles and quantity of food securely inside the dinghy and launch her unmanned, confident that the swell would take her to the beach.

At 2315hrs Miers used a shaded Aldis lamp to signal to Laycock of his intentions, also asking what had happened to the dinghies and for news of the outcome of the raid. In fact, by this time the dinghies had been found in another cave, so Laycock apprised *Torbay* of the fact – although his signal was not understood by Miers. All Miers comprehended was the answer to his question about the raid: 'Goodness only knows,' replied Laycock. 'Some killed in camp and missing from H.Q.' (quoted in PRO 2001: 290).

It was not an encouraging response, and Miers signalled that he could close the beach immediately and have the men evacuated from the beach. Laycock, convinced that the raiders were in no fit state to brave the waves, replied that they would try again the following night. Miers would have preferred to evacuate the men that night, but he had no choice but to accept Laycock's decision, so *Torbay* stood out to sea for the rest of the night.

18 NOVEMBER 1941
2315hrs

***Torbay* signals it**
will return the
next night

Back on the beach the Commandos dispersed in small groups into the caves, where they slept through the hours of darkness while guards patrolled both ends of the beach.

Defending the beach

Laycock was awake an hour before dawn on 19 November and, with Pryor's assistance, he drew up a defensive perimeter for the beach. Three sentries would be posted at the best vantage points looking inland, while their flanks would also be guarded. The rest of the men would remain in the caves until the submarine returned that night. It was also decided that once Laycock's party had finished breakfast, Pryor would organize a relief of the three men who had spent the night at the *wadi* waiting for the return of Cooke and his party.

By the time the raiders had eaten a meagre breakfast, dawn had broken and Pryor could see from his cave an old man ploughing a field with a donkey and a camel half a mile to the west of the beach. A couple of hours later, as Pryor continued to watch the ill-matched ploughing team in amusement, a shot rang out from the sentry posted on the western end of the beach. 'We ran in a fusillade of pops to action stations in a ruined house on a knoll back of our cave,' recounted Pryor.

The *wadi* to the west of the beach at Chescem el-Kelb up which Lt John Pryor and Cpl John Brittlebank advanced in attempt to prevent being encircled by the enemy on the morning of 19 November. In the event Pryor was shot and wounded, and later captured, while Brittlebank was one of the three raiders to escape. (Photograph courtesy Steve Hamilton – Western Desert Battlefield Tours)

I saw our chaps from the cave across the stream running out and taking position likewise, facing west, and there in the distance were some Arabs in red turbans crawling towards us. Everybody fired and they fired back, there were a few bigger bangs that I imagined were from a mortar, and I remember thinking 'our old wall doesn't look a bit bullet proof'. There didn't appear to be many of these native troops as enemy, so we discussed, and thought if we could mop them up, we might still get away in the *Torbay* that night.

Armed with his service revolver and taking the reliable Cpl Brittlebank, Pryor set off with the aim of getting round the seaward side of the enemy. The pair heard the crack of bullets close by as they sprinted across the beach and into the dead ground of a *wadi*. Temporarily concealed from the enemy, Pryor and Brittlebank advanced up the *wadi* towards a stone drinking-trough. Suddenly they came under fire. They ducked, and agreed that the enemy were poor shots. Cautiously, the two men advanced up the *wadi*, using the rocks as cover and relying on the continued inaccuracy of the half-a-dozen Arab soldiers they could see inland. 'Behind the next rock we stopped again in our approach,' recalled Pryor, now within 200 yards of the enemy. 'I looked round and saw that my man [Brittlebank] had managed to get his tommy gun jammed solid. I poked it about a bit and banged it, but couldn't budge it. Rather cross I said "Well try and clear it for God's sake – I'm going on"'.

Pryor went on alone, crouching and running a further 50 yards up the *wadi* towards a cluster of rocks. Once behind the cover of the rocks, Pryor scanned the terrain and saw more Arab soldiers working their way down the scrubland towards the *wadi*. With just his revolver and one grenade, Pryor decided to withdraw back to the beach and tell Laycock what he had seen. A bullet struck a rock just as Pryor dashed out from behind his protection. Then, in the next moment 'something like a horse kicking me up behind bowled me over'. Realizing he'd been hit in the thigh, Pryor crawled down the *wadi* to a flat stone, which he held up like a shield. 'They chipped that twice, and thinks I "if they move a bit they can get me. I must get out," and found my leg would carry me well – which it did back to Bob [Laycock]'.

According to Pryor, when he eventually reached the cave, Laycock's reaction on hearing of the enemy's strength was to curse 'Damn it, that's no good.' In Laycock's account of their discovery, however, he remained unruffled by the presence of 'Carabinieri Arabs known to be stationed at [El] Hania', approximately 8 miles to the west. 'This did not worry us unduly since we were confident that we should be able to drive them off until darkness allowed us to retire to the beach for evacuation, which now seemed feasible as wind and sea were rapidly abating,' wrote Laycock. However, it was soon reported that Germans were now coming down the same *wadi* up which Pryor and Brittlebank had advanced a couple of hours earlier. In addition, the lookouts reported that a large force of Italians was approaching from the north, presumably having overrun the three men left in the *wadi* a mile inland. 'Fairly accurate fire was brought to bear on us, but we were behind good cover and suffered no casualties,' said Laycock.

Although the enemy were not equipped with automatic weapons, they were maintaining a steady advance, and bringing a considerable volume of rifle-fire to bear on and around our position. It was now evident that it would be impossible to hold the beach until dark against such superior forces, and that our only remaining line of retreat would soon be cut off. At about 1400 hours I therefore reluctantly decided to abandon the position and to adopt the alternative plan of hiding in the Jebel until we could rejoin our advancing main forces (the 8th Army). Nothing could be seen of our Western detachment whose original position was now occupied by the enemy and, as a runner sent to reconnoitre, returned with negative information, I presumed that they had been killed or driven off Westwards. I ordered the main body to split into parties of not more than three men each, to make a dash across the open, and to retire through our Eastern detachment to whom they were to pass on my orders.

**19 NOVEMBER 1941
1400hrs**

**Laycock orders
positions to be
abandoned**

Every man for himself

Once in the *Jebel*, the men were told by Laycock to 'adopt' one of three plans: (1) at nightfall return to the beach and swim out to *Torbay*; (2) to make their way to the area of Slonta in which vicinity the Arabs were known to be friendly and where there was a chance of being picked up by the LRDG; (3) to remain hidden in the *Jebel* until the area was overrun by Allied forces.

Leaving Pryor in the hands of an apprehensive medical orderly called Edward Atkins, Laycock disappeared into the scrub and made his way towards the eastern flank, where he found Terry waiting. Together they struck out for the *Jebel*. 'The first half mile of the withdrawal was unpleasant owing to the open nature of the country, but the enemy's marksmanship seems to have been particularly poor, and although we had some close shaves, I do not think we suffered a single casualty since Sergeant Terry and myself would almost certainly have observed any which had occurred,' said Laycock.

Back at the cave the wounded Pryor and Atkins, the medical orderly, waited for the enemy to close, aware that the Arab troops in the pay of the Italians had a reputation for cruelty. Atkins asked Pryor if he thought they would be shot. 'Yes,' replied Pryor, who remembered the medic's 'face

DEFENDING THEIR POSITION (OVERLEAF)

Shortly after dawn the Commandos' position came under attack from a detachment of Libyan troops under Italian command. The enemy, although not carrying automatic weapons, were superior in number to the cornered British and began to work their way towards the caves where they were sheltering. Pryor and Brittlebank attempted to get round the seaward side of the Italians, but in the course of doing so Pryor would be shot in the thigh by a rifle bullet. Here we see the Libyan soldiers advancing on the beleaguered Pryor and Brittlebank, moments before Pryor received his wound.

Vice Admiral H. D. Pridham-Wippell, second-in-command of the Mediterranean Fleet, with Lt-Cdr Miers (right) on the deck of HMS *Torbay* at Alexandria Harbour, 10 May 1942. Miers was awarded the Victoria Cross in March 1942 after a daring action that saw the destruction of two enemy vessels. After the war Miers rose to the rank of rear admiral and was knighted, but following his death in 1985 allegations surfaced linking him to attacks on shipwrecked enemy personnel. (IWM A 10274)

was a picture' as he absorbed the gloomy prediction. In fact the two men were well treated by their captors, with Pryor transported to the Italians' HQ on the back of a mule.

While the Commandos had been fighting a losing battle, *Torbay* had remained submerged, making a reconnaissance of the beaches through the periscope but seeing nothing of the fighting raging in the *wadis* out of sight from the sea. At 1820hrs on 19 November, *Torbay* surfaced, but could see no sign of the Commandos on the beach. By now the weather had eased, and a long swell was running from the north-west straight onto the beach, so Miers instructed Lt Tommy Langton and Sgt Cyril Feebery to go ashore in a folboat. Despite the calmer seas it was still extremely difficult to launch the kayak, but eventually the pair were paddling inshore. 'We rode into the beach on the crest of a wave like a couple of mermaids,' recalled Langton who, like his No. 2, weighed 14 stone.

> The beach was deserted, and after emptying the boat we walked off along the beach toward a light which had appeared on the hillside. This light was the correct colour [blue], but not giving the correct signals, so I was most suspicious of it. After going a little way I thought I saw a movement inland, so we crept towards it but saw nothing further. However, we both heard a shout soon afterwards and since we were by then some distance from our boat and liable to be cut off, I decided to return to it and wait. (Quoted in Pitt 1983: 18)

Something wasn't right – both men sensed it – but neither wanted to return to the submarine without first ensuring they weren't leaving their comrades in the lurch. Langton and Feebery agreed to paddle parallel to the shore towards the blue light. Once abreast of the light, Langton flashed his own white torch and thought he heard a shout in response. Suddenly, a roller crashed into their folboat, capsizing the kayak and causing Langton to lose his Tommy gun in the surf. Even worse, a paddle was lost. 'We crawled along the edge of the surf for a while on hands and knees hunting for the paddle,' said Feebery. 'I had the nasty feeling all the time that someone up there in the trees was staring at my back through the sights of a rifle' (Feebery 2008: 44). Finally admitting defeat in their hunt for the missing paddle, the pair climbed back inside the folboat – which had now sprung a leak – and, relying on the immense strength of Feebery (a former boxing champion), returned to *Torbay*.

Miers spent the rest of the night patrolling the bay at a safe distance, but no further signs were seen from inland. Then, at dawn on 20 November, 'it was seen that all the beaches were in the enemy's hands and they were evidently carrying out a search in which they were being helped by aircraft' (quoted in PRO 2001: 290). *Torbay* remained submerged until the evening, hoping against hope that the enemy had made an unsuccessful sweep of the beach for the Commandos. But the storm had now dissipated, leaving Miers increasingly uneasy 'as the weather … was ideal for E-boat operations' (quoted in PRO 2001: 290) and therefore they risked detection by the Germans. Resolutely remaining off the beach until daylight on 21 November, Miers finally sailed from Chescem el-Kelb at midday, arriving in Alexandria three days later.

By then all but three members of the raiding party had been caught by the Axis forces. John Brittlebank, having lost his officer, Pryor, struck out alone and succeeded in reaching Allied lines 40 days later, on 28 December. (Pryor for a number of years believed that Brittlebank had been killed on the beach.) Three days before Brittlebank reached safety, Laycock and Terry had also made it to the British Eighth Army HQ at Cirene, now in Allied hands. 'Our greatest problem was the lack of food and, though never desperate, we were forced to subsist for periods which never exceeded two and a half consecutive days on berries only, and we became appreciably weak from want of nourishment,' recalled Laycock. 'At other times we fed well on goat and Arab bread, but developed a marked craving for sugar. Water never presented a serious problem, as it rained practically continuously. Our failure to obtain reliable information of the advance of the British forces we found aggravating in the extreme'.

Nevertheless, the pair had made it, a remarkable feat of endurance and initiative that was lauded in the British press. So was the raid itself, immortalized as a glorious example of British pluck, conveniently overlooking the brutal reality that the operation had achieved little other than the death or capture of many brave and well-trained men.

19 NOVEMBER 1941 1820hrs

Torbay surfaces but finds no trace of raiders

21 NOVEMBER 1941

Torbay leaves Chescem el-Kelb for Alexandria

ANALYSIS

On 19 November Lt-Col Geoffrey Keyes was laid to rest in Beda Littoria alongside the four Germans his Commandos had killed: Boxhammer, Jäger, Leutzen and Kovacic. The service was conducted by a Catholic bishop with the Italian garrison and a number of villagers in attendance. Rommel, contrary to some reports, was not present as he had more pressing matters to tackle: namely, Operation *Crusader*, which had commenced on 18 November. Initially all had gone according to plan, Eighth Army advancing 50 miles west across Egypt into Libya, even though the fierce storms that had played havoc with the two special-forces operations also grounded the RAF.

On 21 November, 70th Division launched its breakout from Tobruk, timed to coincide with 7th Armoured Division's drive west, but on the same day a bold counter-thrust from Rommel's 21. Panzer-Division (formerly 5. leichte Division) at Sidi Rezegh occurred. Despite being outnumbered, the Germans defeated the British through superior tactics and actually advanced to within 4 miles of Eighth Army's main supply base. The attempted breakout at Tobruk also failed and Gen Auchinleck responded to the reverse by replacing Lt-Gen Alan Cunningham with Lt-Gen Neil Ritchie on 26 November.

It never occurred to the Germans or the Italians that the purpose of the raid on the villa at Beda Littoria was to 'get Rommel'. One Panzergruppe Afrika diarist wrote on 18 November: 'There is no doubt that the British attack on this Headquarters was for the purpose of capturing important documents'. On the same day General Presti of the Polizia dell'Africa Italiana (PAI, or Libyan Colonial Police) wrote a report on the raid (see overleaf), a copy of which fell into British hands when the Deutsches Afrikakorps withdrew in late December to new defensive positions at El Agheila, west of Beda Littoria.

It was only following the appearance of Laycock and Terry at Cirene on 25 December 1941 that the truth emerged. The British wasted no time in turning what had been an almost utter fiasco into a glorious chapter in military history. Newspapers from Melbourne to Manchester to Massachusetts

25 DECEMBER 1941

Laycock and Terry reach Cirene, now in Allied hands

Lt-Gen Neil Ritchie with his corps commanders, Maj-Gen C. W. M. Norrie (left) and Lt-Gen W. H. E. Gott (right) during the Gazala battles of May–June 1942. Ritchie was deemed to have performed below expectations by his boss, Gen Auchinleck, and was relieved of his command in June 1942; unlike his predecessor, Cunningham, Ritchie returned to senior battlefield command, leading XII Corps in North West Europe in the latter part of World War II. (IWM E 12630)

hailed the pluck of the raiders, with the American press particularly enthusiastic in covering the raid. The United States had joined the war three weeks earlier, and what better way to whip up martial fervour among the American people than with a tale of derring-do?

The Germans were surprised and a little amused to discover the real intention behind the raid. Heinz Schmidt, Rommel's aide-de-camp, described it as a 'fearless exploit by the British … the pity of it from their point of view was that they had been so badly misled' (Schmidt 1951: 98). The villa was not Rommel's HQ, nor had it ever been, and they really should have checked that he was going to be in Africa, let alone Beda Littoria, on the night in question.

So who was responsible for this glaring error? Haselden (who cut communications on the road from Lamluda to El Faidia before safely rendezvousing with the LRDG and returning to the Siwa Oasis) had made the initial reconnaissance of Beda Littoria a few weeks before the raid, but his job was to check the strength of enemy forces in the area. The intelligence already in British hands stated that the villa was Rommel's HQ. Paul Karl Schmidt, the SS officer who wrote the German version of the events during the raid, found it odd that the normally reliable British secret service had blundered so badly. 'Did the Arab agents deliberately deceive the British?' he wondered. 'Was greed on the part of the spies the cause?' Whatever the reason, in September, both in Cairo and London, it was believed that

28 DECEMBER 1941

Brittlebank, the only other survivor, reaches safety

ITALIAN REPORT ON RAID
(TRANSLATION OF A CAPTURED DOCUMENT)

North African Supreme Command General Staff.

Subject: Enemy actions against our L[ine] of C[ommunication] areas.

P.M. 11   18 Nov. 1941

To: The Commissioner of Police at Tripoli, Benghazi, Misurate, Derna and O.C. Libyan Bn. P.A.I. P.M. 27

H.Q. General Staff. North Africa   Inspector General P.A.I. Branch

Following my telegram of even date, the following details will be found useful:

Last night at 0045 hrs. the Intendance Dept. at German H.Q. was surprised by an enemy raiding party who, entering the premises, threw two hand-bombs, which killed two German officers and two soldiers and wounded several others. In the fight which followed, the captain in charge of the party was wounded and a soldier killed [the captain was Robin Campbell and the dead soldier Geoffrey Keyes].

At 0315 hrs. the same night an enemy exploded a bomb under the telephone wire, in between this office and the Cirene crossroads. Immediately afterwards, one of our light cars with a captain aboard was fired on and compelled to stop, though no one was hurt. The British patrol [Lt Roy Cooke's six-man raiding party] then made good its escape, favoured by the darkness and bad weather.

By personal investigation on the spot I ascertained:

(a)   At the Cirene crossroads:

Both officer and chauffeur were unarmed.

The attendants at the petrol distribution post at the crossroads were also unarmed and helpless.

(b)   At the German H.Q. of Beda Littoria:

Both the wounded captain and the soldier who was killed wore a combination suit of burnt coffee colour, short puttees, gym shoes, belt with Colt automatic (British Ordnance issue) and pouch very similar to ours.

Under the combination suit both officers wore civilian clothes.

Documents found on them were: a pocketbook with a pencil plan of German H.Q. and its surroundings in minute detail (down to the motor-car parked in the garden). Two notes of 1000 lire each and several of smaller denominations; a list of 12 English names and the particular job each one of them was to do: 1) kill the sentry; 2) guard the road; 3) put the electric light plant out of action, etc; a letter in Arabic bearing the seal of the noted outlaw Idrises Sanussi [*sic*], recommending the 'people of Cyrenaica to render every aid to our friends', personal letters and photos; maps of Cyrenaica.

I have requested German H.Q. to photograph the Arabic letter, paying particular attention to the seals, and copies will be forwarded on receipt.

After full investigation, supported by the opinion of German H.Q., it would seem to have been a party of British parachutists from a plane which, about 5 days ago, flew for about two hours between Beda and Cirene, dropping some flares.

A Sgt. Major of the Carabinier post at Beda Littoria declares that on the morning of the 17th one of his patrols accosted some 'strangely dressed' soldiers in the Arab market, who replied in German that they belonged to the German Army and who were not arrested for that reason. (Actually, the English captain speaks German well.)

Combining these facts with the landing a few days ago of four British soldiers between Cirene and Derna [Macpherson's reconnaissance patrol that came ashore at Apollonia], the raid by five armoured cars and some lorries south of Buerat El Hassan about two weeks ago [the LRDG patrol commanded by Jake Easonsmith that picked up Haselden], and the news just brought to me of the capture of 16 parachutists and one Italian [members of Stirling's SAS parachute force], forced to land near Tobruk by the machine-gunning of one of our fighter planes, it would appear that:

1. The enemy is attempting to draw troops from the front and spread panic among the people by acts of sabotage and terrorism, brought about by means of coast landings, parachutists and long range raids by motor vehicles along the Southern roads; carried out by the famous 'Commandos' instructed and directed by the Intelligence Service.

2. The native position helps the enemy with shelter and information.

3. The British can go about even in populated centres in civilian clothes or else using a vague sort of uniform such as shorts and shirt with badges hardly visible, etc, so as to foil the police force, who easily mistake them for Germans.

4. There are still too many Italian soldiers who do not seem to realise that it is always necessary to be armed and alert, even in the back areas.

I will not repeat the orders and appropriate instructions already issued, being convinced that Police Commissioners and Battalion Commanders will enforce them and take all measures against surprise, particularly in view of the recent events.

I recommend Bn. Cmdrs to have frequent inspections of sentry posts carried out (sentries might be doubled at night), to have a night patrol under an N.C.O. and also an Air observation post.

Signed: Inspector General P.A.I.

U. PRESTI

Rommel's headquarters were in the prefecture at Beda Littoria. A grave error!' (quoted in Carell 1961: 51).

There were other grave errors made during the planning and execution of the raid. To embark on a mission necessitating a rendezvous with a submarine from a beach at night without a skilled signaller is beyond comprehension. Laycock had given himself a crash course in signalling, but he was nowhere near proficient, as seen by the fact that several of his signals were incomprehensible to Lt-Cdr Miers. The fact Laycock had with him a standard torch and not one with a signalling key also beggars belief.

As previously stated the presence of Laycock on such a small operation, already commanded by a lieutenant-colonel, has never been adequately explained, but both he and Keyes showed poor judgement in pressing ahead with the landings on 15 November in the face of appalling weather conditions. Reading Miers' report on the landings, in which he mentions the 'eagerness of the military to be landed', the inference one draws is that Miers was of the opinion that the operation should not have gone ahead because of the dangerous seas (PRO 2001: 288). It was Miers who strongly advised the following morning against trying to land for a second time the party from *Talisman*, and eventually he ordered Capt Willmott and *Talisman* to return to Alexandria. Thus the operation began with the Commandos

HMS *Talisman* in February 1942. Equipped with ten torpedo tubes and a 4in deck gun, it would return to the Mediterranean and be sunk on 17 September 1942 en route to Malta from Gibraltar. (IWM A 7822)

18 men short of their original number, approximately a third of their potential fighting strength.

As for the raid itself, it was a bungled operation from the moment Keyes led his men through the hedge and into the garden of the villa. Little thought had been given to how they would gain entry to the lightly guarded building, and in the end the courage and presence of mind of the solitary German sentry – Jamatter, armed only with a bayonet – threw the raid into disarray. He should have been killed with a knife by Keyes the moment he opened the door, but Keyes wasn't a ruthless killer; nor was he physically strong, and the German was able to overpower his assailant, alerting the rest of the villa's occupants to the intrusion.

Despite Campbell's assertion that he shot Jamatter with his revolver as he and Keyes grappled in the hallway, the German wasn't among the four fatalities. According to German sources, Jamatter claimed later to have been overpowered by a number of Commandos after his initial struggle with Keyes, and then shot. This had led to speculation that it wasn't Jamatter that Campbell shot, but Keyes by accident.

But whatever happened in those frantic few moments on the ground floor of the villa, the Germans were alerted by the bravery of Jamatter and from that moment the raid was doomed to end in failure. Keyes and the two men with him, Terry and Campbell, could never seriously have hoped to carry out their mission, armed as they were with two revolvers and a Tommy gun. (In April 1944, Anders Lassen and a 12-strong unit of SBS attacked a 40-strong German garrison housed in a two-storey building on the Greek island of Santorini. Using Bren guns and hand grenades they killed half the garrison.) Of course, if the men from *Talisman* had been landed and Keyes had had his full complement of raiders, then they would have been able to attack the villa in strength. Finally, the Commandos' gelignite supplies were damp from the rain and precious minutes were wasted in improvising explosive charges; Keyes should have ensured the explosives were kept dry at all costs despite the heavy storms.

In reality, the raid achieved little in the way of material damage, except the damage caused to the electric light plant by Denis Coulthread and Charlie Bruce's grenade. Contrary to British reports that the dead Germans included three officers, the men killed were not high-ranking members of the German HQ staff. One was a 20-year-old from Bavaria.

Even so, the Panzergruppe Afrika diarist quoted above wrote on 18 November that the 'unexpected sudden death of good comrades has produced a depression which cannot be avoided'. The Italian report on the raid captured the alarm induced by the arrival of British Commandos 250 miles behind their lines, and similar sentiments were expressed in a German intelligence report to Generaloberst Franz Halder, Chef des Generalstabes des Heeres (Army Chief of Staff), on 18 November, in which it said that as a result of the attack 'it is intended to move the [Quartermaster] section of HQ out of Beda … the search for the position of the new headquarters has already been set in motion'.

Rommel (left) consults with Generalmajor Stefan Fröhlich, who as Fliegerführer Afrika led the German air support to the Deutsches Afrikakorps during the winter campaign of 1941/42. Rommel often moved his HQ at short notice during an offensive because he believed commanders needed to be close to the front line in order to react to events rapidly. (Cody Images)

In short, the raiders had inconvenienced the Germans, alarmed the Italians and impressed the Americans. The British turned the Rommel Raid to their advantage, their propaganda boasting that they could strike the Germans when and where they liked. Sgt Terry was awarded a Distinguished Conduct Medal for his role in Operation *Flipper*, the citation praising his courage, leadership and fortitude throughout the mission.

Terry's DCM was thoroughly deserved, but the posthumous Victoria Cross awarded to Geoffrey Keyes was extraordinary yet inevitable. When HM King George VI approved the decoration in 1942, the war was going disastrously for the British in Europe, North Africa and the Far East. The country needed a gallant hero and Keyes, the son of another famous British warrior, fitted the bill. On 16 June 1942 the *London Gazette* announced the award of Keyes' VC, the citation overlooking various unpalatable truths to describe how:

> From the outset Lieutenant-Colonel Keyes deliberately selected for himself the command of the detachment detailed to attack what was undoubtedly the most hazardous of these objectives – the residence and Headquarters of the General Officer Commanding the German forces in North Africa. This attack, even if initially successful, meant almost certain death for those who took part in it.

He led his detachment without guides, in dangerous and precipitous country and in pitch darkness, and maintained by his stolid determination and powers of leadership the morale of the detachment. He then found himself forced to modify his original plans in the light of fresh information elicited from neighbouring Arabs, and was left with only one officer and an N.C.O. with whom to break into General Rommel's residence and deal with the guards and Headquarters Staff.

At zero hour on the night of 17th–18th November, 1941, having despatched the covering party to block the approaches to the house, he himself with the two others crawled forward past the guards, through the surrounding fence and so up to the house itself. Without hesitation, he boldly led his party up to the front door, beat on the door and demanded entrance.

Unfortunately, when the door was opened, it was found impossible to overcome the sentry silently, and it was necessary to shoot him. The noise of the shot naturally aroused the inmates of the house and Lieutenant-Colonel Keyes, appreciating that speed was now of the utmost importance, posted the N.C.O. at the foot of the stairs to prevent interference from the floor above.

Lieutenant-Colonel Keyes, who instinctively took the lead, emptied his revolver with great success into the first room and was followed by the other officer who threw a grenade.

Lieutenant-Colonel Keyes with great daring then entered the second room on the ground floor but was shot almost immediately on flinging open the door and fell back into the passage mortally wounded. On being carried outside by his companions he died within a few minutes.

By his fearless disregard of the great dangers which he ran and of which he was fully aware, and by his magnificent leadership and outstanding gallantry, Lieutenant-Colonel Keyes set an example of supreme self-sacrifice and devotion to duty.

Geoffrey Keyes had finally emerged from the shadow of his father.

THE INAUGURAL SAS RAID

The second special-forces raid authorized by Auchinleck to coincide with the launch of Operation *Crusader* was similarly ill fated. On 15 November 1941, David Stirling and 54 men arrived at the forward landing ground at Bagoush, approximately 200 miles west of Cairo. The same storm that bedevilled Keyes' raiding party as they attempted to come ashore from *Talisman* and *Torbay* ravaged the coastline further east to such a degree that Brig Sandy Galloway, one of Auchinleck's key staff officers, advised Stirling that the mission should be aborted. Dropping by parachute in those wind speeds, and on a moonless night, would be hazardous in the extreme. Stirling absorbed the reports and the advice of Galloway and chose to let his men decide: did they wish to cancel the mission, or press on and to hell with the storm? The SAS chose to press the attack.

Some of the original members of the SAS, who took part in the ill-fated raid of 16/17 November 1941 from which just 21 out of 55 men returned. Undaunted by this terrible setback, David Stirling changed strategy and in the future the SAS approached their target in vehicles, not aircraft. (SAS Regimental Archive)

Stirling divided his force into four sections under his overall command. Jock Lewes was to lead Nos 1 and 2 sections and Blair Mayne would be in charge of sections 3 and 4. At 1830hrs on 16 November a fleet of trucks arrived at the officers' mess to transport the men to the five Bristol Bombay aircraft that would fly them to the target area. Stirling was in the lead aircraft, along with nine other ranks including Sgt Bob Tait, who wrote a report of the raid upon his return some time later:

> We were scheduled to arrive over the dropping area about 2230 hours but

owing to the weather which I think was of gale force, and the heavy A.A. [anti-aircraft] barrage we were much later. The pilot had to make several circles over the area, gliding in from the sea, coming down through the clouds right over Gazala, which was well lit up by flares dropped by the bombing force, covering our arrival. During this glide, we came in for an uncomfortable amount of A.A. We finally were dropped about 2330 hours, and owing to the high wind – I estimated this about 30 miles per hour – we all made very bad landings. I myself being the only one uninjured. Captain Stirling himself sustained injuries about the arms and legs, Sergeant Cheyne, we never saw again. We had considerable difficulty in assembling, the wind having scattered us over a wide area but finally set off at about 0100 hours [on 17 November]. (WO 218/98)

A few hours later Stirling conceded the weather had scuppered their plans and he set a new bearing for the rendezvous, a point near the Rotondo Segnali on a desert track called the Trig al-Abd, 34 miles inland from both Gazala and Tmimi airfields. Also headed for the RV was Blair Mayne's party and the stick commanded by Jock Lewes, both of whom had been defeated by the ferocious storm sweeping across the Western Desert. 'It was extraordinary really that our entire stick landed without injury because the wind when you jumped was ferocious and of course you couldn't see the≈ground coming up,' recalled Johnny Cooper, a member of Lewes' section. Cooper continued:

I hit the desert with quite a bump and was then dragged along by the wind at quite a speed. When I came to rest I staggered rather groggily to me feet, feeling sure I would find a few broken bones but to my astonishment I seemed to have had nothing worse than the wind momentarily knocked out of me. There was a sudden rush of relief but then of course, I looked around me and realised I was all alone and, well, God knows where. (Quoted in Mortimer 2004: 24)

Another member of Lewes' party, Jeff Du Vivier, wrote in his diary:

The lightning was terrific. It continued to pour in buckets for about 30 minutes and by the end of this time we were sitting waist deep in a swirling tide of water. I was shivering, not shaking. All the bones in my body were numbed. I couldn't speak, every time I opened my mouth my teeth just cracked against one another. (Quoted in Mortimer 2004: 25)

In all, just 21 of Stirling's 54 men returned from the raid in the face of what the noted war correspondent Alexander Clifford called 'the most spectacular thunderstorm within local memory' (quoted in Mortimer 2004: 25). On 21 November the LRDG searched an 8-mile front in the hope of picking up any stragglers from the parachute drop, but none was seen. Stirling later discovered that one of the five aircraft had been shot down by a German Messerschmitt, and though most men survived the crash landing they were soon taken into captivity. So, too, was the raiding party under the command of Lt Eoin McGonigal, who had fought with great distinction alongside Geoffrey Keyes at Litani River. McGonigal died of wounds sustained during the landing.

The inaugural SAS raid had ended in disaster, but even as Stirling absorbed the cost of the operation to his unit, an idea was taking root in his head. The seed of the idea was actually planted by Capt David Lloyd-Owen, in command of the LRDG rendezvous party, who suggested over a mug of tea that if parachuting was too hazardous a form of transport in the desert, why not let the LRDG drive the SAS to the target area? Having operated in the region for nearly 18 months they knew the desert intimately, and could not only drop the raiders within marching distance of the target, but pick them up afterwards and avoid detection on the long journey back to base. The following month the LRDG transported a raiding party of seven men led by Paddy Mayne to Tamet aerodrome, where they destroyed 24 aircraft and a barracks full of Axis pilots. In the months that followed the SAS would go from strength to strength, becoming the scourge of the Deutsches Afrikakorps and earning Stirling the sobriquet 'The Phantom Major'. The birth of the SAS legend had begun.

AFTERMATH

German doctors couldn't save Robin Campbell's leg and it was amputated before he was sent to a prisoner-of-war camp. In 1944 he was exchanged for a German prisoner, returning to England where he was the feature of an article in the literary review journal *Horizon* entitled 'A Prisoner Looks Back'. 'On the whole, I would say that captivity had a beneficial effect upon all but the most unteachable,' reflected Campbell, adding: 'I fancy that many people would benefit by a year of enforced inactivity and freedom from small anxieties and distractions to examine their own and others' conduct.' After the war, Campbell became a journalist and artist. He died in 1985, aged 73.

Keyes was disinterred from his resting place in Beda Littoria and reburied in the Allied cemetery at Benghazi. The cross that the Germans had erected was sent back to the Keyes' parish church in Buckinghamshire, where it arrived shortly before Sir Roger Keyes died in his sleep in December 1945.

Rommel, the man Campbell and Keyes had tried to kill, went on to become the army group commander tasked with defending the coastline of Northern France. British special forces would stage another attempt to kill Rommel in the summer of 1944. In June, shortly after the D-Day landings in Normandy, an SAS operation codenamed *Houndsworth* was launched in the Morvan, an area of rolling countryside to the west of Dijon. During the course of the three-month-long operation the SAS commander, Maj Bill Fraser – who had fought alongside Keyes in No. 11 (Scottish) Commando – learned from the local Resistance forces of Rommel's presence at a château at La Roche-Guyon, west of Paris. Fraser communicated the intelligence to the UK and requested permission to launch a daring attack on the château in the hope of killing the *Generalfeldmarschall*.

Instead, a six-man SAS team was assembled and inserted into France between Chartres and Rambouillet in July with orders to kidnap or kill

Opposite: Despite his attempt to kill Rommel, on the orders of the German general Keyes was buried in Beda Littoria, along with the four German soldiers killed during the raid. Keyes was subsequently reburied in the Allied cemetery at Benghazi and the cross that the Germans had erected was sent back to the UK. (Photograph courtesy Steve Hamilton – Western Desert Battlefield Tours)

NOVEMBER 1943

Rommel is appointed C-in-C of Heeresgruppe B

Rommel. But the operation, codenamed *Gaff* and under the command of Lt Jack 'Ramon' Lee, was rendered redundant before the raiders had even set out for the target; instead of being in the château, Rommel was in a hospital, recovering from a fractured skull caused when his car crashed off the road during a strafing attack by an RAF fighter. Implicated in the plot to assassinate Adolf Hitler in the summer of 1944 and given a choice by the Nazi High Command between facing the People's Court and committing suicide, Rommel swallowed a cyanide pill, having been given an assurance his family would not be harmed.

Jack Terry joined the SAS in early 1942 and served with distinction for the rest of the war. After demobilization he returned to Nottinghamshire and joined the police force. Shortly before his death in 2006, Terry broke his silence on the raid, in response to the publication of a book that criticized the operation, and in particular Keyes' role. Though Terry conceded that Keyes might have been shot by Campbell 'by mistake. In a situation like that, things happen', he had this to say about the raid as a whole, in the *Nottingham Evening Post* on 13 August 2004:

Rommel is seen here visiting Hitler's Rastenburg headquarters in spring 1942. He rose to the rank of Generalfeldmarschall and enjoyed an enhanced reputation despite the comprehensive defeat of the Axis forces operating in North Africa in May 1943. (NARA)

In war you have to take opportunities when they arise and Keyes thought he had discovered the opportunity to take out Rommel. If it had succeeded it would have done a lot of good for the Allied campaign in North Africa… No-one can tell me that someone takes more than 50 men on a mission of such incredible danger just to glorify himself. I would not think that's right. Keyes was a good man.

'Up the Blue' was the SAS slang for an operation behind enemy lines. This photo shows three SAS troopers in cheerful spirits, perhaps because the Allies have got Rommel and the Deutsches Afrikakorps on the run. Six months later the war in North Africa would be over. (SAS Regimental Museum)

14 OCTOBER 1944

Rommel commits suicide

BIBLIOGRAPHY

Published sources

Carell, Paul, trans. Mervyn Savill (1961). *The Foxes of the Desert*. New York, NY: Dutton.

Combinedops.com, http://www.combinedops.com/Black%20Hackle.htm (accessed 6 September 2013).

Feebery, Cyril (2008). *Guardsman and Commando: The War Memoirs of RSM Cyril Feebery DCM*. Barnsley: Pen & Sword.

Hare-Scott, Kenneth (1946). 'The Daring Raid on Rommel's H.Q.', *The War Illustrated*, Vol. 10, No. 247, 6 December 1946: 515–16.

Keyes, Elizabeth (1956). *Geoffrey Keyes of the Rommel Raid*. London: George Newnes Ltd.

Lewin, Ronald (1977). *The Life and Death of the Afrika Korps*. London: B.T. Batsford.

Mortimer, Gavin (2004). *Stirling's Men: The Inside History of the SAS in World War II*. London: Weidenfeld & Nicolson.

Mortimer, Gavin (2011). *The SAS in World War II: An Illustrated History*. Oxford: Osprey Publishing.

Mortimer, Gavin (2012). *The Daring Dozen: 12 Special Forces Legends of World War II*. Oxford: Osprey Publishing.

Pitt, Barrie (1983). *The History of the Special Boat Squadron in the Mediterranean*. London: Century Publishing.

Public Records Office (2001). *Special Forces in the Desert War 1940–1943*. London: Public Record Office.

Ross, Hamish (2003). *Paddy Mayne: Lt Col Blair 'Paddy' Mayne, 1 SAS Regiment*. Stroud: Sutton Publishing.

Saunders, H. St G. (1949). *The Green Beret: The Story of the Commandos 1940–45*. London: Michael Joseph.

Schmidt, Heinz (1951). *With Rommel in the Desert*. London: George Harrap & Co.

Sutherland, David (1998). *He Who Dares: Recollections of Service in the SAS, SBS & MI5*. Barnsley: Leo Cooper.

Ziogate, Saiva, Varvounis, Miltiades & Baird, Bob (1999). 'Submarine atrocities'. http://www.oocities.org/pentagon/camp/3166/ (accessed 26 April 2013).

Kew Public Record Office

WO 201/717 – Col Laycock's personal papers
WO 201/718 – Layforce signal equipment
WO 201/720 – Col Laycock's report on Operation *Flipper*
WO 218/98 – Brief history of L Detachment, SAS
WO 218/171 – No. 11 (Scottish) Commando, Layforce

Author interviews

Johnny Cooper, 2002
Jeff Du Vivier, 2003
Albert Youngman, 2011

INDEX

Locators in **bold** refer to illustrations
and captions.